# QUICK GUIDE TO WINNING BLACKJACK

## 30 Minutes to Beating the House

# QUICK GUIDE TO WINNING BLACKJACK

## 30 Minutes to Beating the House

**Avery Cardoza**

**CARDOZA PUBLISHING**

**Visit our web site! www.cardozapub.com**

Cardoza is the foremost gaming and gambling publisher in the world with a library of more than 100 up-to-date and easy-to-read books and strategies. These authoritative works are written by the top experts in their fields and with more than 7,000,000 books in print, represent the best-selling and most popular gaming books anywhere.

To My Extended Family
*Linda, Zachary & Xyzlo*


Second Edition

Copyright©2001, 2004 by Avery Cardoza
-All Rights Reserved-

Library of Congress Catalog Card No: 2003114963
ISBN:1-58042-122-9

Write for your free full color catalogue of gambling and gaming books, advanced, and computer strategies.

## CARDOZA PUBLISHING
PO Box 1500 Cooper Station, New York, NY 10276
Phone (800)577-WINS
e-mail: cardozapub@aol.com
**www.cardozapub.com**

# ABOUT THE AUTHOR

Avery Cardoza is the foremost gambling authority in the world and best-selling author of twenty-one gambling books and advanced strategies, including the encyclopedic *How to Win at Gambling*, and the best selling classic, *Winning Casino Blackjack for the Non-Counter*.

Cardoza began his gambling career underage in Las Vegas as a professional blackjack player beating the casinos at their own game and was soon barred from one casino after another. In 1981, when even the biggest casinos refused him play, he founded Cardoza Publishing, which has sold more than seven million books and published more than 100 gaming titles.

Though originally from Brooklyn, New York, where he is occasionally found, Cardoza has used his winnings to pursue a lifestyle of extensive traveling which has included extended sojourns in exotic locales around the world, and of course, Las Vegas, where he did extensive research into the mathematical, emotional and psychological aspects of winning.

In 1994, he established Cardoza Entertainment, a multimedia development and publishing house, to produce interactive gambling simulations that give players a taste of a real casino; not only with animated and responsive dealers, but with the full scale of bets at the proper odds. The result, *Avery Cardoza's Casino*, featuring 65 gambling variations, became an instant entertainment best-seller making its way onto USA Today's best-seller's list.

Cardoza's most recent project is *Avery Cardoza's PLAYER*, a new and exciting national gambling lifestyle magazine that celebrates the fun, the energy, and the hedonistic pleasures of casino gaming at its best. Every issue of *PLAYER* features writing from the top gambling authorities in the world—the names you know and have come to trust—and loads of content on the lifestyle around gambling. Check out this hot magazine and get a great subscription rate at www.cardozaplayer.com.

# TABLE OF CONTENTS

## I: THE WINNING MIND

## II: WINNING CONCEPTS

## III: THE STRATEGIES

## IV: MONEY MANAGEMENT

## V: THE END STUFF

# INTRODUCTION

I want you to win money at blackjack. That is what this book is about. I am going to make the basics of play and the winning strategies easy to learn and understand, so that in just a few sittings, you will have the skills to beat the casino.

Many of you know that blackjack can be beat, but very few of you actually end up winning. The problem? You never actually understood why the correct plays should be made, what these plays are, and how to put the whole picture together so you walk away a winner.

We'll go through this together, looking at the most important issues of the game, from how much money to bring and how much to bet, to crucial subjects such as limiting losses, maximizing wins, and the most neglected winning requirement of all – managing your emotions.

I'm going to show you what I know in terms you can understand. The operative word here is *easy*. Simplification in life is always the clearest path.

You *can* have fun and win at the same time. The fun part is up to you, leave the winning approach to me.

You want to be a winner? Okay, good. So let's get going.

# THE WINNING MIND

I know all the casino's tricks and I know how they get your money from you. But I also know how to beat them at their own game and what it takes as a player to walk away a winner.

I used to make my money exclusively as a professional blackjack player until no casino in Nevada would allow me to play. Not only was I barred from the little sawdust joints of Northern Nevada, but from the Vegas casinos as well where my photo had been distributed around town.

As a professional blackjack player, as you can understand, that made it tough to survive. No casino wanted to deal blackjack to me. I started resorting to disguises, not just physical ones, but behavioral ones as well. I needed to *act* like a different player, like the rest of the losers frequenting the tables. I studied their habits, picking up ones which best suited my personality, and exaggerating others when it suited the situation.

I often took on the role of a novice, asking beginner questions and using all sorts of tricks I developed – anything that would distract attention from who I really was.

My goal was to win, that is why I was at the table.

### Learning How to Lose

Playing blackjack *professionally* requires nerves of steel to be able to emotionally handle the losing streaks that do occur. That is why there are so few professional players. Most players cannot handle the heat of a couple of beatings. Even I can lose three times in a row. And you know something? It doesn't mean that I will win that fourth time because it is a brand new session. I could lose again.

What separates me from other skilled technical players is not just my extra expertise at the game, it is my ability to emotionally handle losing. In gambling, so to speak, that is what separates the men from the boys. *I know how to lose.* And that is why I know how to win.

Like a successful skier must learn how to fall, a successful gambler must learn how to lose. And that is what you must work on. I have devoted a lot of ink to this concept because it really separates the winners from the losers and I am trying to make a winner out of you.

I've spend thousands and thousands of hours studying every aspect of blackjack, from the minutia of card removal in highly specific situations, card count formula weightings and system design, to dealer habits and betting pattern effects. But more than anything else, I have studied the psychology of the game. This is not a look at whether a player should hit or stand (which of course, is important), but how one *reacts* to the ups and downs in the game.

If someone knows how to beat the game, why doesn't that player win? Why do normally "together" people suddenly lose it at the tables and get wiped out beyond their expectations and means in one bad session? Why do some people seem "destined" to lose, no matter how lucky a particular session may be? How many of you have experienced good winning sessions only to walk away a loser?

The answers to all these questions come from the same cut of cloth, a simple understanding of the inner workings of the mind. It is important to recognize that emotions play a role in winning and losing, a significant role.

## Controlling Your Emotions

Where the situation gets the better of one's emotions, it is the smart player who recognizes this and calls it a day, while the loser continues to play, sucked deeper into a bad situation.

You must understand where the big game is. The *big game* is not on the table my friend. It is in your head.

When you are at the table, are you mentally prepared to play your best game? If the answer is "yes," you are good to go and will give the game your best shot. However, if the answer is "no," for whatever reason, game over, stay away or get away from the table – immediately.

One of my biggest skills as a professional blackjack player is my self control. I can sit down and play for as long as I like. The casino can't tell me I have to play more hands. If I want to leave, I leave. I control *my* environment – how much I bet, how long I play, and what strategies I want to use.

No emotional state of mind ever dictates my actions. I

control the game, the game never controls me.

I always understood this crucial concept and never, not even once in my entire career as a professional blackjack player, did I ever give my mental edge back to the casino. That is what makes me a tough player. I know when I lose my edge and get lost from those tables so fast, the casino doesn't even get one more hand out of me. Not one. I take my blackjack money seriously.

I don't know how you feel, but if I am inclined to donate my hard-earned money, believe me, I have much better places to direct that cash than to a casino.

Understanding and taking control of your emotional state of being is an important concept you won't see discussed in any other book. Many of the gambling authors out there don't really understand this concept (and for that matter, some of these hacks don't even understand the basic playing concepts). Yet there is no more important point you need to learn to be a winner.

But like I said upfront, Avery Cardoza is here to teach you how to win. That is what this book is about.

Nothing I will say in this book about emotional or self-control will be news to you. You know all this already. My goal here is to keep you pointed in the right direction. I want you to beat the casino.

With that said, let's examine what you are doing at the blackjack table and make sure that we're both clear on what your goals are when *your* money is on the line.

## GOAL

The most important first step in a winning approach is to clearly understand your *real* goal of playing. Let's look at four possible motivations for you to be at the blackjack table. I am putting these in question form to prod you into thinking about the answers.

1. Are you there to lose your money?
2. Are you there just to have fun, and winning and losing is unimportant?
3. Are you there to win money?
4. Or are you there to have fun but would like to win?

If you have answered "yes" to either 1 or 2, then you don't need to read this book and are wasting my time and yours. If winning or losing is the same for you either way, you need to get some motivation in life so that things you do take on some meaning.

However, as I suspect must be the answer, you have answered "no" to 1 and 2, but "yes" to either 3 or 4, then we must go about pursuing that winning goal.

So let's restate the goal of what you are doing at the blackjack table and make this clear:

*You are playing blackjack to win money.*

Now that we have that clear and are both on the same page, let's see what I have to do to get you there.

## THE WINNING FORMULA

The winning formula can be simplified into three basic approaches, as follows:

### 1. Understand and Take Control of Your Emotions

This was the theme of this chapter, and its message in various forms will be throughout this book.

### 2. Learn to Play the Basics Strategies Perfectly

Blackjack is a game of percentages, and for a good player, a game of small percentages. You must play perfect basic strategy to have about an even game against the casino.*

### 3. Exercise Strict Money Management Principles

Managing your money, in the form of how much to wager given your disposable gambling money, stop-loss, stop-win strategies and the like, are very important in any winning formula. There will be an entire chapter devoted to these crucial concepts.

* By implementing counting or non-counting techniques (see the Cardoza strategies in the back of the book), you will actually have the edge over the casino - but first, you must thoroughly learn the Basic Strategies presented in this book.

# THE BASICS

Blackjack is a pretty simple game. You get two cards to start, as does the dealer. Your goal is to beat the dealer by either getting a higher total than the dealer without exceeding 21, or if the dealer exceeds 21, winning automatically – as long as you haven't exceeded 21 first.

Going over 21 is called **busting** and is an automatic loser. Busted hands should be turned up immediately. If you bust, your hand is lost, even if the dealer busts as well afterwards. That's your only disadvantage as a player. If the dealer busts, all remaining players, those that have not busted, automatically win their bets.

You are playing to beat the dealer. Other player's point totals and wins and losses are irrelevant to your hand. If you have a higher point total, you win; if the dealer has a higher total, he wins. If you both have the same total, the hand is a tie, called a **push** at blackjack, nobody wins.

The player goes first in blackjack. You can choose from various strategy options, taking one or more additional cards (hitting), taking no more cards (standing), or if the situation is appropriate, doubling down or splitting.

17

We'll come back to the player options in a minute. Let's look at the rest of the basics first.

## The Decks of Cards

Casinos use one, two, four, six and sometimes as many as eight decks of cards in their blackjack games. Often, within the same casino, single and multiple deck games will be offered. Most games outside of Nevada are multiple deck games of at least four decks.

Blackjack played with a single deck of cards is called a **single deck** game, and with two or more decks, is called a **multiple deck** game. Essentially, whether played as single deck or multiple deck, the rules are the same.

When one or two decks are used, the dealer holds the cards in his hand. When more than two decks are used, the cards are dealt from a rectangular plastic or wooden device known as a **shoe**. The shoe is designed to hold multiple decks of cards, and allows the cards to be easily removed one at a time by the dealer.

Each deck used in blackjack is a standard pack of 52 cards, consisting of 4 cards of each value, Ace through King. Suits have no relevance in blackjack. Only the numerical value of the cards count.

In a multiple deck game, the player's cards are typically dealt face up and are not supposed to be handled or touched except by the dealer. In a single deck game, the player's cards are dealt face down and are handled by the player.

Does it matter if your cards are dealt face up?

Strategically, no, because the dealer has no options and must play by the rules of the game, draw to 17 or better, and then stand. I think the game is more fun when the cards are dealt face down, but realistically, it is how you play the cards that is most important, not whether they are face up or face down.

Originally, in the 60s, 70s, and somewhat into the 80's, most of the blackjack games offered were played as single deck affairs. Since the 80's most blackjack games offered use multiple decks dealt out of a shoe.

Multiple deck games became popular for two reasons. First, with less shuffling involved, casinos were able to deal more hands per hour and increase their profits. Second, casinos reasoned that more decks would stop the card counters from getting an edge against them.

Do multiple decks stop card counters as casinos intended? Not at all. It is a common misconception that it is hard for a player to count cards in a multiple deck game. On the contrary, the skills necessary to beat the multiple deck game are no different than what is needed for a single deck one! (We'll talk more about card counting and non-counting strategies later.)

**Card Values**
Each card in the deck is counted at face value; a 2 equals two points, a 3 equals three points, and a 9 equals nine points. The face cards, Jack, Queen and King, are counted as 10 points. Thus, there are four ranks worth 10 points - the 10, Jack, Queen, and King - which makes a total of 16 ten value cards in the deck.

The Ace can be counted as 1 point or 11 points, at your discretion. When the Ace is counted as 11 points, that hand is called **soft**, as in the hand Ace, 7, *soft 18*. All other totals, including hands where the Ace counts as 1 point, are called hard, as in the hand 10, 6, A, *hard 17*.

## PAYOFFS
Other than the player blackjack described below, all bets are paid off at even money – for every dollar bet, you will win an equal amount if your hand is a winner. Thus, if you have a $25 bet on the table and win, you receive the original $25 back along with the $25 in winnings for a total of $50.

## BLACKJACK - AUTOMATIC WINNER
If the original two card hand contains an Ace with any 10 or face card (J, Q, K), the hand is called a **blackjack** and is an automatic winner for you. When you get a blackjack, it pays 3-2 on your bet!

Thus, if you have $10 bet, you'll get back $15 in winnings along with your original $10 for a total of $25.

The dealer, on the other hand, only gets even money when he gets a blackjack, not the 3-2 bonus you get. While a dealer's blackjack is an automatic winner for the casino, you'll lose *only* the bet you have on the table.

If you could trade off blackjacks with the casino all day long, you would make a fortune getting paid 3-2 on your blackjacks while the casino only got even money. If only things were so easy!

If both the dealer and you are dealt a blackjack, the hand is a push, nobody wins.

In games where you hold the cards, make sure to turn your blackjacks over immediately.

## DEALER'S RULES

The dealer must play by prescribed guidelines. He must draw to any hand 16 or below and stand on any total 17-21. When the rules state that the dealer must stand on all 17's, he will count his Ace as 11 points if that gives him a hand totaling 17 to 21. Otherwise the Ace will be counted as 1 point.

In some casinos the rules dictate that the dealer must draw on soft 17. In these casinos, the dealer's Ace will count as 1 point when combined with cards totaling 6 points, for example, A, 2, 3, soft 17, and the dealer will have to draw until he forms a hand of at least a *hard* 17.

The dealer has no playing options and cannot deviate from these rules.

## PLAYER OPTIONS

Unlike the dealer, you can vary your strategy as you like. After receiving your first two cards, you have the following options:

### 1. Drawing (Hitting)

If you are not satisfied with your two card total you have the option to draw additional cards. Where both your cards are dealt face up, the typical manner in which multiple deck games are played, you are not supposed to touch the cards. To ask for a card, either scratch the felt with your index finger or point toward the cards if you desire an additional card.

In a single deck game, where the cards are held in your hand, you indicate to the dealer that you want another card by scraping the felt surface with your cards. The motion is almost like scratching your body, except that you are scratching the felt layout (not your skin, of course!) with the cards.

## 2. Standing

When you are satisfied with your hand and do not wish to draw additional cards, you can choose to stand. When the cards are dealt face up, you indicate this decision to the dealer by waving your hand palm down over the cards. In a single deck game, where you actually hold the cards, you indicate this decision by sliding your cards face down under your bet.

## 3. Doubling Down

This option allows you to double your original bet after receiving your original two cards. You will receive one card and only one card, which you must take. That card will form your final hand. If you had bet $25, doubling down allows you to add an additional $25 to that bet, for a total bet of $50.

In games where the cards are dealt face up, to double down, you simply place the additional bet next to your original one. This indicates to the dealer that you are doubling down. To double down in a single deck game, turn your cards face up, and place them in front of your bet.

Now, place an additional bet equal to the original bet so that there are two equal stacks side by side.

The dealer will then deal one card face down, usually slipping that card under your bet. You may look at that card if you so desire. In games where both player cards are dealt face up, this card is usually dealt face up.

## 4. Splitting Pairs

If dealt a pair of identical value cards, such as 3-3, 7-7, 8-8 (any combination of 10, J, Q, K is considered a pair), you can split these cards so that two separate hands are formed.

In games where both your cards are dealt face up, the split is indicated by placing the additional bet next to the original one, and after, using hand signals as above to indicate hitting or standing.

To split a pair in a single deck game, turn the pair face up, separating them so that one card is in front of the original bet and the other card is next to it, a few inches to its side. Then place a bet equal to the original bet behind the second card. Each hand is now played separately, using finger and hand signals to indicate hitting and standing decisions.

If the first card dealt to either split hand has a value identical to the original split cards, that card may be split again (resplit) into a third hand, and even a fourth hand if yet another identical card is drawn. Paired aces are an exception. When you split Aces, you receive only one card on each Ace and may not draw again, no matter what card is drawn. Note that a 10 card drawn to a split Ace is only a 21 with the normal even-money payout. It is not considered a blackjack.

## 5. Doubling Down After Splitting

This option, which allows you to double down on one or both of the hands resulting from a split, is not often found in Nevada casinos, though it is standard in Atlantic City. As in normal doubling, you may only double down on the original two cards of the split hand.

Doubling after splitting works as follows. Let's say you get dealt a pair of 7s and split them, drawing a 4 to the first one for an 11, and a 3 to the second one for a 10. You may elect to double down on both the 11 and the 10, playing each as a separate hand according to the normal doubling procedures.

## 6. Surrender (Late Surrender)

You may "surrender" the original two card hand and forfeit one half of your bet after it has been determined that the dealer does not have a blackjack. Surrender is offered in only a few casinos.

To surrender your hand, simply, inform the dealer that you are surrendering your hand. The dealer will collect the cards and take one half of the bet.

## 7. Early Surrender

This very favorable option was originally introduced in Atlantic City but is no longer offered there. This option allows you to surrender your hand and lose half the bet *before* the dealer checks for a blackjack.

### 8. Insurance

If the dealer shows an Ace as his upcard, he will ask you if you want insurance. If you exercise this option, you are in effect betting that the dealer has a 10-value card as his hole card, a blackjack. It is a separate bet altogether.

To take insurance, place up to one-half the amount of your original bet in the area marked "insurance." If the dealer does indeed have a blackjack, you get the insurance bet back and your original bet stays intact. If the dealer does not have a blackjack, your insurance bet is lost and play will continue with your original bet still being active.

### "Even Money" Blackjack

If you hold a blackjack and take insurance on the dealer's Ace, you will end up with an even-money payoff whether the dealer has a blackjack or not. Suppose you have a $10 bet and take insurance for $5 on your blackjack. If the dealer has a blackjack, you'll win 2 to 1 on your $5 insurance bet but push on your blackjack. If the dealer doesn't have a blackjack, you lose the $5 insurance bet but get paid 3-2 on the blackjack. Either way, you end up with the same $10.

You'll sometimes see this at the table where a player will flip over his cards and announce to the dealer, "even money."

## INSURANCE STRATEGY

Beginners and even experienced players love to take insurance. Well, guess what. It's a bad bet. In fact it is a really bad bet that gives the casino an 8% edge!

Unless you are a card counter with knowledge of the ten richness in the deck, insurance is always a bad bet, regardless of the hand you may hold.

Since the insurance payoff is 2-1, this wager will only be profitable for you when the ratio of 10s to other cards is either equal to or less than 2-1. A full deck has 36 non-tens and 16 tens, a ratio greater than 2 to 1, therefore an awful percentage play for you.

## INSURING A BLACKJACK

Taking insurance when you have a blackjack is also a bad bet, despite the well-intentioned advice of dealers and other players to always "insure" a blackjack. Remember, insurance is a separate bet and has nothing to do with the two cards you hold whether those cards are a blackjack or a lousy 16. Either way, you don't want insurance.

## THE PLAY OF THE GAME

The dealer will shuffle the cards and offer the full stack to one of the players to cut. The **cut** occurs when you remove the top portion of the deck and place it next to the original stack. The dealer will complete the cut by placing the new stack on top of the original pile, effectively restacking the deck. The cut is a traditional protection against dealer cheating.

The dealer now removes one or more of the top cards, called **burn cards**. In single and double deck games, the burn cards are either put under the deck face up, where all subsequent cards will be placed or face down into the **discard rack,** a plastic holder designed to hold cards.

You must make your bets before the cards are dealt. If you forget to do so, the dealer will remind you that a bet is due.

You have the option, if you choose, to sit out a hand or two without betting while maintaining your seat. I have done this often. The casinos don't like it but don't worry about what they like or don't like. It's your money. The dealer will ask if you want to play and you can inform him that you will be sitting this hand out.

The dealer deals clockwise from his left to his right, one card at a time, until each player and the dealer have received two cards. Your cards will usually be dealt face down in a single or double deck game, though it makes no difference if they are dealt face up as they usually are in multiple deck games dealt out of a shoe, for the dealer is bound by strict rules from which he cannot deviate.

The dealer deals only one of his two cards face up. This card is called an **upcard**. The face down card is known as the **hole card** or the **downcard**.

If the dealer's upcard is an Ace, he will ask you if you want insurance. If you opt to take insurance, place a bet of up to one-half their wager in the area marked "insurance." This is located on the layout above your bet.

If the dealer has a blackjack, all players that did not take insurance lose their bets. Players that took insurance break even on the play. If the dealer doesn't have a blackjack, he collects the lost insurance bets and play continues.

The procedures vary when the dealer shows a 10-value card. In many Nevada casinos the dealer must check his hole card for an Ace. If he has a blackjack, it is an automatic winner for the house. All player bets are lost. (Players can't insure against a 10-value card.) Players that hold a blackjack push on the play. If the dealer doesn't have a blackjack, he will face the first player and await that player's decision.

In Atlantic City and some overseas casinos, the dealer will only check his hole card after all players have acted.

Play begins with the bettor on the dealer's left, in the position known as **first base**.

You have the option to stand, hit, double down, split (if you have two cards of equal value) or surrender (if allowed). You may draw cards until you are satisfied with your total or bust, or you may exercise one of the other options discussed previously.

Play moves to the next player. If a player busts (goes over 21) or receives a blackjack, he must turn over his cards immediately. If a bust, the dealer will collect the lost bet. If a blackjack, the dealer will pay 3-2 on the won bet.

After the last player has acted upon his cards, the dealer will turn his hole card over so that all players can view both of his cards. He must play his hand according to the strict guidelines regulating his play; drawing to 17, then standing. If the dealer busts, all players still in the game for that round of play win automatically.

After playing his hand, the dealer will turn over each player's cards in turn, going counterclockwise from his right to his left, the opposite direction from how he dealt, paying the winners, and collecting from the losers. Once a bettor has played his hand, he shouldn't touch his cards again. He should let the dealer expose his hand which the dealer will do once he has played out his own hand.

When the round has been completed, all players must place a new bet before the next deal.

## CASINO PERSONNEL

The casino employee responsible for the running of the blackjack game is called the **dealer**. The dealer's duties are to deal the cards to the players and play out his own hand according to the rules of the game. He converts money into chips for players entering the game or buying in for more chips during the course of the game, makes the correct payoffs for winning hands, and collects bets from the losers.

The dealer's supervisor – technically called the **floorman**, but more commonly referred to as the **pit boss** – is normally responsible for the supervision of between 4-6 tables. He makes sure the games are run smoothly and he settles any disputes that may arise with a player. More importantly, his job is to oversee the exchange of money and to correct any errors that may occur.

## ENTERING A GAME

Just sit down and play baby. Find yourself any unoccupied seat at a blackjack table and make yourself comfortable. Place the money you wish to gamble with near the betting box in front of you and inform the dealer that you would like to get some chips for your cash. Chips may be purchased in various denominations so let the dealer know which chips or combination of chips you'd like if you have a particular preference.

The dealer will take your money and call out the amount he is changing so that a supervisor is aware that a transaction is taking place and can supervise that exchange.

Casinos prefer that you use chips for betting, for the handling of money at the tables slows down the game. Though cash can be used to make a bet, all payoffs will be in chips. The casinos never pay winning hands with cash.

To bet, place your chips (or cash) in the betting box directly in front of you. All bets must be placed before the cards are dealt.

## CASINO CHIPS
Standard denominations of casino chips are $1, $5, $25, $100 and for the high rollers, $500, $1,000 and even higher denomination chips are sometimes used. Though some casinos use their own color code, the usual color scheme of chips are: $1–silver, $5–red, $25–green and $100–black.

## TRAVELER'S CHECKS & MONEY ORDERS
At the tables, only cash and chips are accepted, so if you bring traveler's checks, money orders and the like, you must go to the area of the casino marked **Casino Cashier** to get these converted to cash. Be sure to bring proper identification to insure a smooth transaction.

## HOUSE LIMITS

Placards located at either corner of the table indicate the minimum and maximum bets allowed at a particular table. Within the same casino you may find minimums raging from $1, $2 and $5, to other tables that require the players to bet at least $25 or $100 per hand.

At the $1, $2 and $5 tables, the house maximum generally will not exceed $500 to $1,000 while the $25 and $100 tables may allow the players to bet as high as $3,000 a hand or higher.

## PRIVATE TABLES

The casino will normally supply any high roller with a private table if he requests it. If you are a big money player and prefer your own table, let the pit boss know that you wish to have your own table. If your betting amounts meets the casino's requirements, the casino will try to accommodate you.

## CASHING OUT

Dealers turn cash into chips. They will not change your chips back into cash. To get those chips converted back into cash, you'll need to go to the cashier's cage which is typically located at the rear of the casino. (They want to give you the opportunity to drop some coins in the slots on the way.)

## TIPPING

**Tipping**, or **toking**, as it is called in casino parlance, is totally at your discretion, and in no way should be considered an obligation. It is not your duty to support casino employees, that is the casino's job.

If you toke, toke only when you're winning, and only to dealers that are friendly and helpful to you. Do not toke dealers that you don't like or ones that try to make you feel guilty about not tipping. Dealers that make playing an unpleasant experience for you deserve nothing.

The best way to tip a dealer is to place a bet for the dealer in front of your own bet, so that his chances of winning that toke are tied up with your hand. If the hand is won, you both win together; if the hand is lost, you lose together. By being partners on the hand, you establish camaraderie with the dealer.

Naturally, he or she will be rooting for you to win. This is the best way to tip, for when you win, the dealer wins double – the tip amount you bet plus the winnings from that bet.

## CHEATING

It is my belief that cheating is not a problem in the major American gambling centers, though I would not totally eliminate the possibility. If you ever feel uncomfortable about the honesty of a game, stop playing. Though you probably are being dealt an honest game, the anxiety of being uncomfortable is not worth the action.

Do not confuse bad luck with being cheated, or a dealer's mistake as chicanery. Dealers have a difficult job and work hard. They are bound to make honest mistakes. If you find yourself shorted on a payoff, bring it immediately to the dealer's attention and the mistake will be corrected.

## FREE DRINKS AND CIGARETTES

Casinos will offer you unlimited free drinking while playing at the table. In addition to alcoholic beverages, you can order milk, soft drinks, juices or any other beverages. This is ordered through and served by a cocktail waitress.

Cigarettes and cigars are also complimentary and can be ordered through the cocktail waitress.

# CASINO RULES

Blackjack can be found all over the world, and though basically the same wherever played, the rules and variations vary from casino to casino and sometimes, they even vary within a casino itself.

**Nevada Rules**
The Las Vegas Strip rules are among the best in the world and can give you a slight edge on the single deck game if our strategies are followed. The rule exceptions noted in Downtown Las Vegas and in Northern Nevada games are slightly disadvantageous, but these can easily be overcome by using the winning techniques presented later.

**Las Vegas Strip Rules**
   • Dealer must draw on all totals of 16 or less, and stand on all totals of 17-21.
      • Player may take insurance on a dealer's Ace.
      • Insurance payoffs are 2 to 1.
      • Player receives a 3 to 2 payoff on his blackjack.
      • Player may double down on any initial two card combination.
      • Identical pairs may be split, resplit, and drawn to as desired with the exception of split Aces, on which the player is allowed only one hit on each Ace.
      • One, two, four and bigger deck games are standard.

## Downtown Las Vegas Rules

The downtown area of Las Vegas centers around Fremont street and contains clubs such as the Horseshoe, the Golden Nugget, and the Golden Gate. Downtown has more of a local feel with smaller, friendlier casinos. Rules are the same as the Las Vegas Strip rules with one exception:

• Dealer must draw to soft 17.

## Northern Nevada Rules

The Northern Nevada area includes Lake Tahoe and Reno, along with many small gambling towns. The rules are the same as Las Vegas Strip rules with two exceptions:

• Dealer must draw to soft 17.
• Doubling is restricted to two card totals of 10 and 11 only.

## Atlantic City Rules

The New Jersey Casino Control Commission regulates the rules and variations allowed in Atlantic City casinos, and Atlantic City clubs must abide by the following guidelines:

• Dealer must draw to all totals 16 or less, and stand on all totals of 17-21.
• Player may take insurance on a dealer's Ace. Insurance payoffs are 2 to 1.
• Player receives a 3 to 2 payoff on his blackjack.
• Player may double on any initial two card combination.
• Identical pairs may be split but not resplit.
• Doubling after splitting allowed.
• Four, six and eight decks are standard.

## Single and Multiple Deck Games

Note that single deck blackjack is hard to find or nonexistent outside the Nevada casinos. Multiple deck blackjack is the predominant style of play in casinos around the world and the type of game you'll most likely face when you take on the casinos at blackjack.

# THE DEALER'S UPCARD

The high density of tens in the deck, the ten factor, makes a natural separation of the dealer's upcard into two distinct groupings: 2s through 6s, the dealer "stiff" or "busting" cards, and 7s through As (Aces), the dealer "pat" cards.

The former group, the stiff cards 2-6, are the weak dealer cards that will allow you to play more aggressively due to their high busting potential. The latter group, the pat cards 7-Ace, are the dealer's stronger upcards since they tend to make more hands, and of course, in the case of the 9, 10s, and Ace, better hands.

We'll look at each group in turn, starting with the busting cards.

### THE BUSTING CARDS: DEALER'S UPCARD 2-6
The busting cards, consisting of dealer upcards of 2-6, are the weakest the dealer can hold. The high prevalence of 10s in the deck, along with other high cards, give these upcards a high busting potential, and as you know, when the dealer busts, it's a win for you, providing of course, that you haven't busted out yourself.

While you have a losing expectation anytime you are dealt

a hard total of 12-16, you never chance busting against these dealer upcards (with the exception of the 12 vs. 2-3 exceptions where you hit), hoping instead to carry the day defensively on their high busting potential.

On the other hand, when you are dealt strong totals with possibilities for doubling and splitting, you get on the offense with aggressive plays to take advantage of the dealer's weaknesses.

### Dealer Shows a 5 or 6

These are the cards you want to see the dealer holding hand after hand. They are the weakest of all the dealer upcards and you will play your most aggressive game against them, doubling and splitting hands at every profit-able opportunity. The dealer will bust about 43% of the time showing these weak cards. Never, ever, take a chance of busting out your total when you're looking at a dealer's 5 or 6. In other words, whenever you hold a hard 12 or higher, stand - always.

### Dealer Shows a 4

The dealer's 4 is not quite as weak as the 5 or 6, but with an average bust rate of about 40%, it is a card you will go after with all your aggressive plays. Like the 5 and 6 above, be very happy when the dealer lays down that 4.

### Dealer Shows a 3

There is still a relatively high busting potential to the dealer's hand, but with so many more cards that will make him a hand as well, consider the 3 to be a more dangerous card.

### Dealer Shows a 2

With one less card that will bust the dealer (compared to the 3), this is the most dangerous of the dealer busting cards. You may be surprised to learn that the dealer will make an 18 or better slightly more than half the time showing the 2. Typically, you will not chance busting any hard total of 12-16 against a dealer's bust card, however, when you hold a 12 (with fewer chances yourself of busting), draw against the dealer's upcard of 2 and 3.

## THE PAT CARDS: DEALER'S UPCARD 7-ACE

The strength of these upcards vary depending upon the particular upcard the dealer is showing. However, the one overriding principle is that since you expect the dealer to make a hand, you must try to make one yourself. Thus, it is never correct to stand with any hard total of 12-16 against these strong dealer upcards.

Against the dealer's 7-Ace, you will be less aggressive in doubling and splitting situations. The dealer has too much firepower with these upcards and you will play aggressively against them only with your best hands.

### Dealer Shows an Ace

This is the card of double jeopardy. First, you must get by the blackjack, however, once you do (if you do), you are looking at the dealer upcard with the least chance of busting – just 17% of the time, or about one in every six hands. That's the bad news. The good news is that while the dealer makes a lot of hands, they tend to be weaker hands than when the dealer has the 10 as an upcard, so if you hold a powerful hand yourself, like a 19 or 20, you are actually in good shape.

### Dealer Shows a 10 Value Card

The first thing to realize in this situation is that the dealer has very good chances of making a strong hand. If nothing else, he will make a hand of 17 or better approximately 75% of the time, which is three out of every four hands. That means he will bust out only 25% of the time, one out of four hands. With such a low busting percentage, you must draw to improve when you have your busting totals of 12-16, or you stand very little chance of winning.

So when you are thinking about standing with those 15's or 16's, think again. Automatically giving up three out of four hands is too steep a price to pay.

The dealer upcard of 10 (J, Q, and K) makes the strongest totals of all the dealer upcards. Any of the dealer downcards of 7 or higher will automatically make a pat hand, while one of the many 10 value cards will of course make a powerful 20 – a hard hand to beat. Smaller downcards of 2-6 aren't necessarily doom for the dealer's hand as a portion of these, with a favorable draw, can turn into a good hand as well.

All told, a 10 value card is not the card you want the dealer to show as an upcard, but given the vast number of them in the deck, you can expect to see them about one in three hands (four out of every thirteen times to be exact).

### Dealer Shows a 9

If you're holding a 20 (and certainly a 21), you love looking at the dealer's 9 – you're in good shape here. If you have a 19, while you would rather see the dealer hold a 7 or 8, you're still feeling pretty good. However, if you're sitting with a 17 or 18, then you're less than pleased because the 9 represents a more powerful hand, and if your hand is even worse, a 12-16, you'll need to draw to improve because that 9 won't be busting very often.

## Dealer Shows an 8
You're feeling better now, unless you hold a bust hand of 12-16, where you are the underdog, or a hard 17, which is a doomed hand against the 8. Any hand of 18 or better obviously leaves you in a good position to push with the 18, or win, with the 19 or higher total.

## Dealer Shows a 7
The dealer will make a lot of hands with a 7, but they tend to be hands that are easily beat. If you could give the dealer a 7 every time out, you could probably bankrupt a casino in under 24 hours. On the Las Vegas Strip, dealers must stand on all 17s, which is favorable to the player, while in Downtown Las Vegas, dealer's must draw to soft 17s, a rule which is unfavorable to you, for as we talked about above, you would love to stick the dealer with a 17 all day long.

# PLAYER TOTALS

We've looked at the general strengths and weaknesses of the dealer cards, now let's get a better understanding of the player totals.

### The Hand of 21
The strongest hand you can hold. As a two card total, it is a blackjack with a very nice 3-2 bounty. On a 21 made with more than two cards, while it is not a blackjack, you have the best hand possible and cannot possibly lose. Obviously, you never hit a 21.

### The Hand of 20
An excellent hand that has big winning expectations against all dealer upcards. You're in great shape here.

### The Hand of 19
Again, this is a very strong hand with winning expectations against all dealer upcards including the 10. If you could get dealt 19's all day long, you would be a very happy blackjack player.

### The Hand of 18
Here is a surprise: 18's are not very good hands, they are only *okay* hands. Unlike the 19's, which would be winners, if you get dealt 18's all day long, you are going to

lose money since the average dealer total is slightly higher than an 18. Now that you understand that 18's are just decent totals, and not really strong as most players think, you will get a better understanding of some of the Basic Strategy plays.

### The Hand of 17

Hands of hard 17 are just plain lousy. This total is not okay, it plain stinks, and will lose a lot of money for you in the long run. When your total of 17 is hard, there is not a blessed thing you can do to improve it since every card drawn of 5 or higher will bust you. That is why you must stand with all hard 17's, whether you like it or not. But when the total of 17 points is soft, as in an Ace and a 6 or an Ace 2 4, for two examples, you will never stand, no matter what the dealer shows as an upcard.

### Hands of Hard 12-16

These are your busting hands, hands which will be busted by any 10 value card. You have a long term losing situation and can only hope for the best. The problem here is that you have to go first, and if you bust, you're out regardless of what happens to the dealer afterwards.

If you stand, which is the best play when the dealer shows a 2-6, you will lose money, winning only the times that the dealer busts, approximately 35-43% of the time (depending upon the upcard itself). But that is a far superior play than drawing.

When the dealer shows a pat card, 7 or higher, the situation becomes even worse. The dealer is not going to bust very often, which means that if you do not draw, you will be giving up lots of hands. You must risk the draw and the possibility of busting to give yourself a fighting chance. It is a far better play to try to improve the total of hard 12-16 to a point total of 17 or better.

As you see, hard totals of 12-16 are not good hands for you, but if you want to emerge as a winner, you need to minimize the losses on these bad hands by playing the correct Basic Strategy.

## Hands of 11 or Less

You can never bust with any of these hands, and can only improve. Always draw a card when you hold hard 11 or less, unless of course, doubling or splitting, as recommended by the Basic Strategy charts in this book, are a favorable option.

## Putting it All Together

We'll now turn our attention to the actual strategies that must be played at the tables. There are different strategies, as you will see, for the single deck game and for the multiple deck game. The subtle differences between the two strategies are due to the fact that removal of the three cards we know, our two cards and the dealer's upcard, affect the remaining 49 cards in a single deck game but are barely felt in the larger multiple deck packs.

Let's move on to the Basic Strategies!

# THE BASIC STRATEGY

When the cards are dealt, you are given a situation and a choice. You have knowledge of the two cards you have been dealt as well as the dealer's upcard. (We will assume knowledge of no other cards in the deck.) You have a decision to make. Should you hit, stand, double down, and if appropriate or possible, take insurance, split or surrender? These decisions affect your chances of winning the hand.

Assuming this knowledge of only your two card hand and the dealer's upcard, there is only one mathematically correct way to play your hand against the dealer. This is called the **Basic Strategy**.

The following chapters go over the Basic Strategies you must follow to give yourself the best chances of beating the dealer. While all strategies will be shown from the perspective of the multiple deck player, since these are the most popular games found, the single deck exceptions will be noted.

Master Charts of the Basic Strategies for both single and multiple deck games will be included in the Master Charts chapter.

# HITTING & STANDING HARD TOTALS

We'll start out with the easiest and most basic plays in blackjack, the hitting and standing strategies. You should be familiar with these in no time. First, we'll show the basic strategy chart, which is identical for both single deck and multiple deck games, then go over the basic principles and explanations for the strategies.

At the end of this chapter, there will be a short quiz so you can get all the plays down cold.

| Hitting & Standing - Hard Totals | | | | | | | | | | |
|---|---|---|---|---|---|---|---|---|---|---|
|  | 2 | 3 | 4 | 5 | 6 | 7 | 8 | 9 | 10 | A |
| 11/less | H | H | H | H | H | H | H | H | H | H |
| 12 | H | H | S | S | S | H | H | H | H | H |
| 13 | S | S | S | S | S | H | H | H | H | H |
| 14 | S | S | S | S | S | H | H | H | H | H |
| 15 | S | S | S | S | S | H | H | H | H | H |
| 16 | S | S | S | S | S | H | H | H | H | H |
| 17-21 | S | S | S | S | S | S | S | S | S | S |

**H** = Hit    **S** = Stand

## GENERAL STRATEGY

### Playing Hard 17-21
Stand against all dealer upcards.

### Playing Hard Hands 11 or Less
Unless choosing a doubling or splitting option, draw against all dealer upcards. There is no risk of busting and it never makes sense to stand pat.

### Playing the Hard 12's-16s
These are the problem hands, because drawing a card can bust our hand and make it an automatic loser. The following principles apply:

1. Whenever the dealer has a bust card showing, a 2-6, stand on all hard totals of 12 or more. Do not bust against a dealer stiff card. Exception - Hit 12 vs. 2, 3. Our 12 can only be busted by a ten card, and the dealer has more chances to get a hand with a 2 or 3 as an upcard.

2. When the dealer shows a 7, 8, 9, 10 or A, hit all hard totals of 16 or below (unless doubling or splitting is more profitable – in any case, always draw a card). Whenever the dealer has a pat card showing, a 7-Ace, he is likely to make a hand, so we must always try to improve to at least a 17.

Let's test your knowledge now on a short quiz.

# QUIZ #1
## HITTING AND STANDING - HARD TOTALS

Hitting and standing with hard totals are the most basic plays in blackjack. There is no excuse for you to not know these answers cold.

If you're unclear about any answer, you need to study the charts more. Fill in your answers below.

| # | Player Hand | Dealer Upcard | Correct Play |
|---|---|---|---|
| 1. | 6  K | 7 | _____ |
| 2. | 2  10 | 6 | _____ |
| 3. | 8  7 | Q | _____ |
| 4. | 3  4 | 10 | _____ |
| 5. | J  K | 6 | _____ |
| 6. | J  J | 6 | _____ |
| 7. | K  3 | 2 | _____ |
| 8. | 9  7 | K | _____ |
| 9. | 7  10 | 10 | _____ |
| 10. | 7  10 | A | _____ |
| 11. | Q  5 | 2 | _____ |
| 12. | K  2 | 3 | _____ |

# QUIZ #1
## ANSWERS

| # | Player Hand | Dealer Upcard | Correct Play |
|---|---|---|---|
| 1. | 6  K | 7 | Hit |
| 2. | 2  10 | 6 | Stand |
| 3. | 8  7 | Q | Hit |
| 4. | 3  4 | 10 | Hit |
| 5. | J  K | 6 | Stand |
| 6. | J  J | 6 | Stand |
| 7. | K  3 | 2 | Stand |
| 8. | 9  7 | K | Hit |
| 9. | 7  10 | 10 | Stand |
| 10. | 7  10 | A | Stand |
| 11. | Q  5 | 2 | Stand |
| 12. | K  2 | 3 | Hit |

# SOFT TOTAL PLAYS

Soft totals are hands where the Ace is counted as 11 points, such as the hand A5 or A32, both of which can be counted as 6 points or 16 points, at your discretion.

Soft totals sometimes give you a second chance for a good hand. For example, against a dealer's upcard of 9 on an Ace 5, soft 16 hand, the draw of a 10 doesn't knock you out as it would if you started with a hard 16. The 10 now gives you a hard 16 and another chance to draw since the Ace would be counted as a 1. If another draw brings a 4, this second chance allowed you to get a probable winning hand of 20.

| SOFT TOTAL PLAYS | | | | | | | | | | |
|---|---|---|---|---|---|---|---|---|---|---|
| | 2 | 3 | 4 | 5 | 6 | 7 | 8 | 9 | 10 | A |
| A2-A3 | H | H | H* | D | D | H | H | H | H | H |
| A4-A5 | H | H | D | D | D | H | H | H | H | H |
| A6 | H* | D | D | D | D | H | H | H | H | H |
| A7 | S | D | D | D | D | S | S | H | H | H |
| A8 | S | S | S | S | S | S | S | S | S | S |
| A9 | S | S | S | S | S | S | S | S | S | S |

**H** = Hit          **S** = Stand          **D** = Double

*Double A2 vs. 4 and A3 vs. 4 in a single deck game.
*Double A6 vs. 2 in a single deck game.

## GENERAL STRATEGY

Except on your most powerful hands of 19 and 20, and sometimes the 18, you will always draw more cards with soft totals, either as a straight hit trying to improve, or as a doubling strategy, trying to maximize your advantage.

Doubling with soft totals is generally a gain against weak dealer upcards. The 10 factor figures strongly in the dealer's chances of busting, while on the other hand, the drawing of small and medium cards will often improve your hand to a competitive and winning total.

## INDIVIDUAL HANDS

### Player's Hand of Soft 19 and 20 (A8 and A9)

Stand against all dealer upcards. These are already good solid hands.

### Player's Hand of Soft 18 (A7)

Take advantage of the weakest dealer upcards of 4-6 and the 3 as well, but stand against the dangerous 2. Also stand against the 7 and 8, where your 18 is strong against the dealer's projected 17 and 18. Your 18 is not all that strong so you must try to improve against these powerful upcards.

### Player's Hand of Soft 17 (A6)

Always draw on soft 17 no matter what the dealer shows as an upcard, except against the weakest dealer upcards, where you will double down.

### Player's Hand of Soft 13-16 (A2-A5)

Unless you are able to double down, you should always draw a card to these hands. Standing is a poor option, for these totals will win only when the dealer busts.

# QUIZ #2
## SOFT HANDS STRATEGY

The answers to these strategy plays will depend on whether you are playing a single or multiple deck game. Answers for both will be on the following page.

See if you can do well here. These questions are tricky.

| #   | Player Hand | Dealer Upcard | Correct Play |
| --- | ----------- | ------------- | ------------ |
| 1.  | A  3        | 2             | _____        |
| 2.  | A  7        | 6             | _____        |
| 3.  | A  7        | Q             | _____        |
| 4.  | A  2        | 3             | _____        |
| 5.  | A  5        | 6             | _____        |
| 6.  | A  6        | 2             | _____        |
| 7.  | A  7        | 3             | _____        |
| 8.  | A  8        | 5             | _____        |
| 9.  | A  7        | A             | _____        |
| 10. | A  5        | 4             | _____        |
| 11. | A  5        | 2             | _____        |
| 12. | A  9        | 6             | _____        |

# QUIZ #2
## ANSWERS

| # | Player Hand | Dealer Upcard | Correct Play |
|---|---|---|---|
| 1. | A 3 | 2 | Hit |
| 2. | A 7 | 6 | Double |
| 3. | A 7 | Q | Hit |
| 4. | A 2 | 3 | Hit |
| 5. | A 5 | 6 | Double |
| 6. | A 6 | 2 | Hit* |
| 7. | A 7 | 3 | Double |
| 8. | A 8 | 5 | Stand |
| 9. | A 7 | A | Hit |
| 10. | A 5 | 4 | Double |
| 11. | A 5 | 2 | Hit |
| 12. | A 9 | 6 | Stand |

*Double down in a single deck game

# DOUBLING DOWN HARD TOTALS

This is a profitable option that allows you to double your bet when you have an edge. We covered doubling plays with the soft totals, hands where an Ace was held, now you'll learn the doubling strategies with hard totals.

We'll present the chart for multiple deck doubling first, and after, the one for single deck doubling.

| DOUBLING DOWN - MULTIPLE DECK | | | | | | | | | | |
|---|---|---|---|---|---|---|---|---|---|---|
|        | 2 | 3 | 4 | 5 | 6 | 7 | 8 | 9 | 10 | A |
| 8/less |   |   |   |   |   |   |   |   |    |   |
| 9      |   | D | D | D | D |   |   |   |    |   |
| 10     | D | D | D | D | D | D | D | D |    |   |
| 11     | D | D | D | D | D | D | D | D | D  |   |
| A2     |   |   |   | D | D |   |   |   |    |   |
| A3     |   |   |   | D | D |   |   |   |    |   |
| A4     |   |   | D | D | D |   |   |   |    |   |
| A5     |   |   | D | D | D |   |   |   |    |   |
| A6     |   | D | D | D | D |   |   |   |    |   |
| A7     |   | D | D | D | D |   |   |   |    |   |
| A8-A9  |   |   |   |   |   |   |   |   |    |   |

**D** = Double Down    **Blank** = Do Not Double Down

## Single Deck Doubling

You'll notice that the doubling strategies for single deck play are more aggressive than the multiple deck game, a difference we'll discuss a little later on. There are seven doubling plays we would make in a single deck game that we would not make in a multiple deck one.

|            | Multiple Deck | Single Deck |
|------------|---------------|-------------|
| 8 vs. 5    | Hit           | Double      |
| 8 vs. 6    | Hit           | Double      |
| 9 vs. 2    | Hit           | Double      |
| 11 vs. Ace | Hit           | Double      |
| A2 vs. 4   | Hit           | Double      |
| A3 vs. 4   | Hit           | Double      |
| A6 vs. 2   | Hit           | Double      |

### DOUBLING DOWN - SINGLE DECK

|        | 2 | 3 | 4 | 5 | 6 | 7 | 8 | 9 | 10 | A |
|--------|---|---|---|---|---|---|---|---|----|---|
| 62     |   |   |   |   |   |   |   |   |    |   |
| 44/53  |   |   |   | D | D |   |   |   |    |   |
| 9      | D | D | D | D | D |   |   |   |    |   |
| 10     | D | D | D | D | D | D | D | D |    |   |
| 11     | D | D | D | D | D | D | D | D | D  | D |
| A2     |   |   | D | D | D |   |   |   |    |   |
| A3     |   |   | D | D | D |   |   |   |    |   |
| A4     |   |   | D | D | D |   |   |   |    |   |
| A5     |   |   | D | D | D |   |   |   |    |   |
| A6     | D | D | D | D | D |   |   |   |    |   |
| A7     |   | D | D | D | D |   |   |   |    |   |
| A8-A9  |   |   |   |   |   |   |   |   |    |   |

**D** = Double Down     **Blank** = Hit, Do Not Double Down

## GENERAL STRATEGY

The doubling plays are limited to the hands of 9, 10 and 11, with the 8 added as a weapon for a single deck game. These are strong doubling hands due to the large number of ten value cards in the deck.

You also don't double down with any hard totals 12 or over, not with the high possibility of being busted by a ten value card!

Let's take a quick look at the doubling hands.

### Doubling 11

This is the most powerful doubling hand. In the long run, you will make a lot of money on this hand. Being dealt an 11 should always be welcome news.

Double against all dealer upcards in a single deck game but not against the 11 in a multiple deck game.

### Doubling 10

This is the second strongest doubling hand and will also make you lots of money in the long run.

Double the 10 against the dealer's 2 through 9. Simply hit against the dealer's 10 or Ace. The doubling strategy on the 10 is identical for both single deck and multiple deck.

### Doubling 9

Double 9 against the dealer bust cards of 3 through 6 and draw against all other upcards. In a single deck game, double down against the dangerous 2 as well. Do not double down against any of the dealer pat cards.

### Doubling 8

Do not double down with an 8 in a multiple deck game. Drawing a 10 only gives you an 18, a fair hand that is not good enough to put extra money on the table with.

However, due to the removal of three small cards from the deck, doubling 8 against the 5 and 6 is a valid play in a single deck game.

# QUIZ #3
## HARD DOUBLING STRATEGY

These are potential doubling plays where your choices are to double down, hit or stand. Give these some thought, as they are important plays.

What's it going to be: hit, stand or double down?

| #   | Player Hand | Dealer Upcard | Correct Play |
| --- | ----------- | ------------- | ------------ |
| 1.  | 5  2        | 6             | _____        |
| 2.  | 4  5        | 7             | _____        |
| 3.  | 6  5        | 10            | _____        |
| 4.  | 8  2        | 9             | _____        |
| 5.  | 8  2        | 10            | _____        |
| 6.  | 6  3        | 2             | _____        |
| 7.  | 7  4        | 5             | _____        |
| 8.  | 9  3        | 6             | _____        |
| 9.  | 8  3        | A             | _____        |
| 10. | 3  5        | 4             | _____        |
| 11. | 6  4        | A             | _____        |
| 12. | 2  9        | 2             | _____        |

# QUIZ #3
## ANSWERS

| # | Player Hand | Dealer Upcard | Correct Play |
|---|---|---|---|
| 1. | 5  2 | 6 | Hit |
| 2. | 4  5 | 7 | Hit |
| 3. | 6  5 | 10 | Double |
| 4. | 8  2 | 9 | Double |
| 5. | 8  2 | 10 | Hit |
| 6. | 6  3 | 2 | Hit* |
| 7. | 7  4 | 5 | Double |
| 8. | 9  3 | 6 | Stand |
| 9. | 8  3 | A | Hit* |
| 10. | 3  5 | 4 | Hit |
| 11. | 6  4 | A | Hit |
| 12. | 2  9 | 2 | Double |

*Double down in a single deck game

# SPLITTING

Whenever you have two cards of the same rank, your first thought must go to splitting. The chart below shows splitting situations for the multiple deck game. This is identical to the single deck strategy except for two plays, as noted below:

|  | Multiple Deck | Single Deck |
|---|---|---|
| 22 vs. 3 | Hit | Split |
| 66 vs. 2 | Hit | Split |

## SPLITTING PAIRS

|  | 2 | 3 | 4 | 5 | 6 | 7 | 8 | 9 | 10 | A |
|---|---|---|---|---|---|---|---|---|---|---|
| 22 |  | H* | spl | spl | spl | spl |  |  |  |  |
| 33 |  |  | spl | spl | spl | spl |  |  |  |  |
| 44 |  |  |  |  |  |  |  |  |  |  |
| 55 |  |  |  |  |  |  |  |  |  |  |
| 66 | H* | spl | spl | spl | spl |  |  |  |  |  |
| 77 | spl | spl | spl | spl | spl | spl |  |  |  |  |
| 88 | spl | spl | spl | spl | spl | spl | spl | spl | spl | spl |
| 99 | spl | spl | spl | spl | spl |  | spl | spl |  |  |
| AA | spl | spl | spl | spl | spl | spl | spl | spl | spl | spl |

spl = Split          **Blank** = Do Not Split

**H\*** = Hit in Multiple Deck, Split in Single Deck

Do not split 44, 55, 10s.   Always split 88, AA

## GENERAL STRATEGY

Splitting can do two valuable things. It can turn one poor total into two stronger hands, such as splitting a very weak 16 (8-8) into two decent hands of 8 each, and it allows you to double your money in situations where you have an advantage over the casino.

### Splitting 22 and 33

Split 33 vs. dealer 4 through 7 in a multiple deck game and against the 3 through 7 in a single deck one. The high busting probabilities of the dealer 4, 5 and 6 makes these excellent splits. While splitting against the 7 will not make you money, it does achieve some gain. Do not split against the dangerous dealer's 2, or against the much stronger 8, 9, 10 or Ace. Don't make one loser into two losers.

*Atlantic City and games with doubling after splitting allowed: split 22 and 33 vs. 2 through 7.

### Splitting 44

Do not split 44*. The hard total of 8 gravitates toward a total of 18, a far better position than two weak starting totals of 4 each.

*Atlantic City and games with doubling after splitting allowed: split 44 vs. 5 and 6. The added possibilities of being able to double our bet should either or both of the split totals pull well makes this split an advantageous move.

### Splitting 55

Never split 55. 55 by itself is an excellent doubling hand of 10 against upcards of 2-9. Do not break up this powerful player total into two terrible hands of 5 each.

### Splitting 66

Split 66 against the weak dealer stiff cards 3 through 6. Single deck players can also double against the dangerous 2. You have a losing hand against all dealer upcards as a 12 or as two hands of 6 each. The goal here, however, is to minimize losses. The high dealer busting factor makes splitting 66 against the dealer stiffs a slight gain.

Do not split 66 against the dealer pat cards. You don't need two hands of 16 against cards that will bust only one time in four.

*Atlantic City and games with doubling after splitting allowed: split 66 vs. 2-6.

### Splitting 77

Split 77 against dealer upcards of 2-7. Against the dealer stiff cards 2 through 6, two playable hands of 7 and 7 are preferable to one stiff total of 14 due to the high busting rate of the dealer stiff cards.

Splitting 77 against the dealer's 7 is also an excellent split, for you are taking one losing total of 14 into two potential pushes of 17 each. Do not split 77 vs. the dealer's 8-Ace; you do not want to take one potential loser into two.

### Splitting 88

Split 88 against all dealer upcards. Against the dealer's 2 through 8, you are taking one terrible hand of 16 into two playable totals of 8 each. Splitting 88 against the dealer's 9, 10, A are weak splits, but they do produce a gain over drawing to the terribly weak hard 16.

### Splitting 9s

Split 99 against the weak dealer stiff cards of 2-6, but stand against the 7 – you have the dealer's potential 17 beat! Split against the 8 and 9. Against the dealer's 8, your potential 19 is a big gain, and against the dealer's 9, you don't want to be sitting with only an 18. Against the powerful 10 and Ace, you don't want to turn one potential loser into two. Note that the starting total of 18 is only "fair," not a powerful total like a 19 or 20.

### Splitting 10,10

Do not split 10s. You've won, leave it at that.

### Splitting AA

Split AA against all dealer upcards. This is a huge gain.

---

## ATLANTIC CITY & GAMES
## WITH DOUBLING AFTER SPLITTING ALLOWED

Pairs are split more aggressively to take advantage of doubling situations that may arise as a consequence of a split.

|     | 2   | 3   | 4   | 5   | 6   | 7   | 8   | 9   | 10  | A   |
|-----|-----|-----|-----|-----|-----|-----|-----|-----|-----|-----|
| 22  | spl | spl | spl | spl | spl | spl |     |     |     |     |
| 33  | spl | spl | spl | spl | spl | spl |     |     |     |     |
| 44  |     |     |     | spl | spl |     |     |     |     |     |
| 66  | spl | spl | spl | spl | spl |     |     |     |     |     |
| 77  | spl | spl | spl | spl | spl | spl |     |     |     |     |
| 88  | spl | spl | spl | spl | spl | spl | spl | spl | spl | spl |
| 99  | spl | spl | spl | spl | spl |     | spl | spl |     |     |
| AA  | spl | spl | spl | spl | spl | spl | spl | spl | spl | spl |

**spl** = Split             **Blank** = Do Not Split
Do not split 55, 10s.       Always split 88, AA

# QUIZ #4
## SPLITTING STRATEGY

No doubling after splitting in this quiz. You can always split two identically ranked cards, but should you? It takes a while to learn these plays. Let's see how you do.

Do you split or do something else here?

| # | Player Hand | Dealer Upcard | Correct Play |
|---|---|---|---|
| 1. | 8 8 | 7 | _____ |
| 2. | 8 8 | 2 | _____ |
| 3. | 5 5 | 6 | _____ |
| 4. | 3 3 | 4 | _____ |
| 5. | 2 2 | 7 | _____ |
| 6. | 9 9 | 7 | _____ |
| 7. | A A | A | _____ |
| 8. | 7 7 | 2 | _____ |
| 9. | 9 9 | A | _____ |
| 10. | J Q | 6 | _____ |
| 11. | 7 7 | 7 | _____ |
| 12. | 6 6 | 7 | _____ |

# QUIZ #4
## ANSWERS

| # | Player Hand | Dealer Upcard | Correct Play |
|---|---|---|---|
| 1. | 8  8 | 7 | Split |
| 2. | 8  8 | 2 | Split |
| 3. | 5  5 | 6 | Double! |
| 4. | 3  3 | 4 | Split |
| 5. | 2  2 | 7 | Split |
| 6. | 9  9 | 7 | Stand |
| 7. | A  A | A | Split |
| 8. | 7  7 | 2 | Split |
| 9. | 9  9 | A | Stand |
| 10. | J  Q | 6 | Stand |
| 11. | 7  7 | 7 | Split |
| 12. | 6  6 | 7 | Hit |

# QUIZ #5
## SPLITTING STRATEGY

There are so many splitting situations, that we're going to give you another set of 12. Again, no doubling after splitting. When you can get these right, you are getting good.

Ready to try again? Let's go!

| #   | Player Hand | Dealer Upcard | Correct Play |
| --- | ----------- | ------------- | ------------ |
| 1.  | 4  4        | 3             | _____      |
| 2.  | 8  8        | A             | _____      |
| 3.  | 7  7        | 6             | _____      |
| 4.  | 9  9        | 10            | _____      |
| 5.  | 9  9        | 2             | _____      |
| 6.  | 2  2        | 2             | _____      |
| 7.  | 3  3        | 8             | _____      |
| 8.  | 7  7        | A             | _____      |
| \9. | 4  4        | 7             | _____      |
| 10. | J  J        | 5             | _____      |
| 11. | 9  9        | 8             | _____      |
| 12. | 2  2        | 4             | _____      |

# QUIZ #5
## ANSWERS

| # | Player Hand | Dealer Upcard | Correct Play |
|---|---|---|---|
| 1. | 4  4 | 3 | Hit |
| 2. | 8  8 | A | Split |
| 3. | 7  7 | 6 | Split |
| 4. | 9  9 | 10 | Stand |
| 5. | 9  9 | 2 | Split |
| 6. | 2  2 | 2 | Hit |
| 7. | 3  3 | 8 | Hit |
| 8. | 7  7 | A | Hit |
| \9. | 4  4 | 7 | Hit |
| 10. | J  J | 5 | Stand |
| 11. | 9  9 | 8 | Split |
| 12. | 2  2 | 4 | Split |

# SINGLE DECK MASTER CHARTS

In this chapter, I put the single deck strategies together in individual master charts for easy reference. Single deck games are always the best to play, but they are not often found.

(Since Atlantic City doesn't offer single deck blackjack, there are no single deck charts here – those charts will be in the Multiple Deck Master chart chapter.)

---

**How to Read the Master Charts**

In these charts, the dealer upcard is shown horizontally on the top row, going left to right, and the player's hand, going vertically, up and down, on the left side. Where both intersect in the matrix, there will be a letter or letters to indicate the correct strategy play.

---

## NORTHERN NEVADA SINGLE DECK

Doubling is allowed on 10 and 11 only so you won't be doubling on soft totals or hands of less than hard 10.

|  | 2 | 3 | 4 | 5 | 6 | 7 | 8 | 9 | 10 | A |
|---|---|---|---|---|---|---|---|---|---|---|
| 7/less | H | H | H | H | H | H | H | H | H | H |
| 8 | H | H | H | H | H | H | H | H | H | H |
| 9 | H | H | H | H | H | H | H | H | H | H |
| 10 | D | D | D | D | D | D | D | D | H | H |
| 11 | D | D | D | D | D | D | D | D | D | D |
| 12 | H | H | S | S | S | H | H | H | H | H |
| 13 | S | S | S | S | S | H | H | H | H | H |
| 14 | S | S | S | S | S | H | H | H | H | H |
| 15 | S | S | S | S | S | H | H | H | H | H |
| 16 | S | S | S | S | S | H | H | H | H | H |
| A2 | H | H | H | H | H | H | H | H | H | H |
| A3 | H | H | H | H | H | H | H | H | H | H |
| A4 | H | H | H | H | H | H | H | H | H | H |
| A5 | H | H | H | H | H | H | H | H | H | H |
| A6 | H | H | H | H | H | H | H | H | H | H |
| A7 | S | S | S | S | S | S | S | H | H | H |
| A8 | S | S | S | S | S | S | S | S | S | S |
| A9 | S | S | S | S | S | S | S | S | S | S |
| 22 | H | spl | spl | spl | spl | spl | H | H | H | H |
| 33 | H | H | spl | spl | spl | spl | H | H | H | H |
| 66 | spl | spl | spl | spl | spl | H | H | H | H | H |
| 77 | spl | spl | spl | spl | spl | spl | H | H | H | H |
| 88 | spl | spl | spl | spl | spl | spl | spl | spl | spl | spl |
| 99 | spl | spl | spl | spl | spl | S | spl | spl | S | S |
| AA | spl | spl | spl | spl | spl | spl | spl | spl | spl | spl |

**H** = Hit        **S** = Stand        **D** = Double        **spl** = Split
Do not split 44, 55 (double on 55) and 10s.
Always split 88 and AA.

## LAS VEGAS SINGLE DECK

Las Vegas rules allow for doubling on any two card total.

|        | 2   | 3   | 4   | 5   | 6   | 7   | 8   | 9   | 10  | A   |
|--------|-----|-----|-----|-----|-----|-----|-----|-----|-----|-----|
| 7/less | H   | H   | H   | H   | H   | H   | H   | H   | H   | H   |
| 62     | H   | H   | H   | H   | H   | H   | H   | H   | H   | H   |
| 44/53  | H   | H   | H   | D   | D   | H   | H   | H   | H   | H   |
| 9      | D   | D   | D   | D   | D   | H   | H   | H   | H   | H   |
| 10     | D   | D   | D   | D   | D   | D   | D   | D   | H   | H   |
| 11     | D   | D   | D   | D   | D   | D   | D   | D   | D   | D   |
| 12     | H   | H   | S   | S   | S   | H   | H   | H   | H   | H   |
| 13     | S   | S   | S   | S   | S   | H   | H   | H   | H   | H   |
| 14     | S   | S   | S   | S   | S   | H   | H   | H   | H   | H   |
| 15     | S   | S   | S   | S   | S   | H   | H   | H   | H   | H   |
| 16     | S   | S   | S   | S   | S   | H   | H   | H   | H   | H   |
| A2     | H   | H   | D   | D   | D   | H   | H   | H   | H   | H   |
| A3     | H   | H   | D   | D   | D   | H   | H   | H   | H   | H   |
| A4     | H   | H   | D   | D   | D   | H   | H   | H   | H   | H   |
| A5     | H   | H   | D   | D   | D   | H   | H   | H   | H   | H   |
| A6     | D   | D   | D   | D   | D   | H   | H   | H   | H   | H   |
| A7     | S   | D   | D   | D   | D   | S   | S   | H   | H   | H   |
| A8     | S   | S   | S   | S   | S   | S   | S   | S   | S   | S   |
| A9     | S   | S   | S   | S   | S   | S   | S   | S   | S   | S   |
| 22     | H   | spl | spl | spl | spl | spl | H   | H   | H   | H   |
| 33     | H   | H   | spl | spl | spl | spl | H   | H   | H   | H   |
| 66     | spl | spl | spl | spl | spl | H   | H   | H   | H   | H   |
| 77     | spl | spl | spl | spl | spl | spl | H   | H   | H   | H   |
| 88     | spl | spl | spl | spl | spl | spl | spl | spl | spl | spl |
| 99     | spl | spl | spl | spl | spl | S   | spl | spl | S   | S   |
| AA     | spl | spl | spl | spl | spl | spl | spl | spl | spl | spl |

**H** = Hit    **S** = Stand    **D** = Double    **spl** = Split
Do not split 44, 55 (double on 55) and 10s.
Always split 88 and AA.

75

# MULTIPLE DECK MASTER CHARTS

These are the charts you will use most often since black-jack is generally found only as a multiple deck game. Note that blackjack is played in many places other than the rule centers shown here, however, since these rules typically are based on one of the jurisdictions covered in this chapter, you can use the appropriate charts here for playing a correct strategy.

## Single and Multiple Deck Blackjack Differences
Except for the following changes in the doubling and splitting strategies, multiple deck basic strategy for the basic Las Vegas game is identical to the single deck strategy.

|            | Multiple Deck | Single Deck |
|------------|---------------|-------------|
| 8 vs. 5    | Hit           | Double      |
| 8 vs. 6    | Hit           | Double      |
| 9 vs. 2    | Hit           | Double      |
| 11 vs. Ace | Hit           | Double      |
| A2 vs. 4   | Hit           | Double      |
| A3 vs. 4   | Hit           | Double      |
| A6 vs. 2   | Hit           | Double      |
| 22 vs. 3   | Hit           | Split       |
| 66 vs. 2   | Hit           | Split       |

## NORTHERN NEVADA MULTIPLE DECK

Less aggressive play due to doubling allowed on 10 and 11 only and the multiple deck setting.

|        | 2   | 3   | 4   | 5   | 6   | 7   | 8   | 9   | 10  | A   |
|--------|-----|-----|-----|-----|-----|-----|-----|-----|-----|-----|
| 7/less | H   | H   | H   | H   | H   | H   | H   | H   | H   | H   |
| 8      | H   | H   | H   | H   | H   | H   | H   | H   | H   | H   |
| 9      | H   | H   | H   | H   | H   | H   | H   | H   | H   | H   |
| 10     | D   | D   | D   | D   | D   | D   | D   | D   | H   | H   |
| 11     | D   | D   | D   | D   | D   | D   | D   | D   | D   | H   |
| 12     | H   | H   | S   | S   | S   | H   | H   | H   | H   | H   |
| 13     | S   | S   | S   | S   | S   | H   | H   | H   | H   | H   |
| 14     | S   | S   | S   | S   | S   | H   | H   | H   | H   | H   |
| 15     | S   | S   | S   | S   | S   | H   | H   | H   | H   | H   |
| 16     | S   | S   | S   | S   | S   | H   | H   | H   | H   | H   |
| A2     | H   | H   | H   | H   | H   | H   | H   | H   | H   | H   |
| A3     | H   | H   | H   | H   | H   | H   | H   | H   | H   | H   |
| A4     | H   | H   | H   | H   | H   | H   | H   | H   | H   | H   |
| A5     | H   | H   | H   | H   | H   | H   | H   | H   | H   | H   |
| A6     | H   | H   | H   | H   | H   | H   | H   | H   | H   | H   |
| A7     | S   | S   | S   | S   | S   | S   | S   | H   | H   | H   |
| A8     | S   | S   | S   | S   | S   | S   | S   | S   | S   | S   |
| A9     | S   | S   | S   | S   | S   | S   | S   | S   | S   | S   |
| 22     | H   | H   | spl | spl | spl | spl | H   | H   | H   | H   |
| 33     | H   | H   | spl | spl | spl | spl | H   | H   | H   | H   |
| 66     | H   | spl | spl | spl | spl | H   | H   | H   | H   | H   |
| 77     | spl | spl | spl | spl | spl | spl | H   | H   | H   | H   |
| 88     | spl | spl | spl | spl | spl | spl | spl | spl | spl | spl |
| 99     | spl | spl | spl | spl | spl | S   | spl | spl | S   | S   |
| AA     | spl | spl | spl | spl | spl | spl | spl | spl | spl | spl |

**H** = Hit          **S** = Stand          **D** = Double          **spl** = Split

Do not split 44, 55 (double on 55) and 10s.
Always split 88 and AA.

78

## LAS VEGAS MULTIPLE DECK

The multiple deck game makes you less aggressive on seven doubling and two splitting situations.

| | 2 | 3 | 4 | 5 | 6 | 7 | 8 | 9 | 10 | A |
|---|---|---|---|---|---|---|---|---|---|---|
| 7/less | H | H | H | H | H | H | H | H | H | H |
| 8 | H | H | H | H | H | H | H | H | H | H |
| 9 | H | D | D | D | D | H | H | H | H | H |
| 10 | D | D | D | D | D | D | D | D | H | H |
| 11 | D | D | D | D | D | D | D | D | D | H |
| 12 | H | H | S | S | S | H | H | H | H | H |
| 13 | S | S | S | S | S | H | H | H | H | H |
| 14 | S | S | S | S | S | H | H | H | H | H |
| 15 | S | S | S | S | S | H | H | H | H | H |
| 16 | S | S | S | S | S | H | H | H | H | H |
| A2 | H | H | H | D | D | H | H | H | H | H |
| A3 | H | H | H | D | D | H | H | H | H | H |
| A4 | H | H | D | D | D | H | H | H | H | H |
| A5 | H | H | D | D | D | H | H | H | H | H |
| A6 | H | D | D | D | D | H | H | H | H | H |
| A7 | S | D | D | D | D | S | S | H | H | H |
| A8 | S | S | S | S | S | S | S | S | S | S |
| A9 | S | S | S | S | S | S | S | S | S | S |
| 22 | H | H | spl | spl | spl | spl | H | H | H | H |
| 33 | H | H | spl | spl | spl | spl | H | H | H | H |
| 66 | H | spl | spl | spl | spl | H | H | H | H | H |
| 77 | spl | spl | spl | spl | spl | spl | H | H | H | H |
| 88 | spl | spl | spl | spl | spl | spl | spl | spl | spl | spl |
| 99 | spl | spl | spl | spl | spl | S | spl | spl | S | S |
| AA | spl | spl | spl | spl | spl | spl | spl | spl | spl | spl |

**H** = Hit    **S** = Stand    **D** = Double    **spl** = Split
Do not split 44, 55 (double on 55) and 10s.
Always split 88 and AA

## ATLANTIC CITY MULTIPLE DECK

More frequent pair splitting due to Doubling after Splitting rules leads to a more aggressive splitting strategy.

|        | 2   | 3   | 4   | 5   | 6   | 7   | 8   | 9   | 10  | A   |
|--------|-----|-----|-----|-----|-----|-----|-----|-----|-----|-----|
| 7/less | H   | H   | H   | H   | H   | H   | H   | H   | H   | H   |
| 8      | H   | H   | H   | H   | H   | H   | H   | H   | H   | H   |
| 9      | H   | D   | D   | D   | D   | H   | H   | H   | H   | H   |
| 10     | D   | D   | D   | D   | D   | D   | D   | D   | H   | H   |
| 11     | D   | D   | D   | D   | D   | D   | D   | D   | D   | H   |
| 12     | H   | H   | S   | S   | S   | H   | H   | H   | H   | H   |
| 13     | S   | S   | S   | S   | S   | H   | H   | H   | H   | H   |
| 14     | S   | S   | S   | S   | S   | H   | H   | H   | H   | H   |
| 15     | S   | S   | S   | S   | S   | H   | H   | H   | H   | H   |
| 16     | S   | S   | S   | S   | S   | H   | H   | H   | H   | H   |
| A2     | H   | H   | H   | D   | D   | H   | H   | H   | H   | H   |
| A3     | H   | H   | H   | D   | D   | H   | H   | H   | H   | H   |
| A4     | H   | H   | D   | D   | D   | H   | H   | H   | H   | H   |
| A5     | H   | H   | D   | D   | D   | H   | H   | H   | H   | H   |
| A6     | H   | D   | D   | D   | D   | H   | H   | H   | H   | H   |
| A7     | S   | D   | D   | D   | D   | S   | S   | H   | H   | H   |
| A8     | S   | S   | S   | S   | S   | S   | S   | S   | S   | S   |
| A9     | S   | S   | S   | S   | S   | S   | S   | S   | S   | S   |
| 22     | spl | spl | spl | spl | spl | spl | H   | H   | H   | H   |
| 33     | spl | spl | spl | spl | spl | spl | H   | H   | H   | H   |
| 44     | H   | H   | H   | spl | spl | H   | H   | H   | H   | H   |
| 66     | spl | spl | spl | spl | spl | H   | H   | H   | H   | H   |
| 77     | spl | spl | spl | spl | spl | spl | H   | H   | H   | H   |
| 88     | spl | spl | spl | spl | spl | spl | spl | spl | spl | spl |
| 99     | spl | spl | spl | spl | spl | S   | spl | spl | S   | S   |
| AA     | spl | spl | spl | spl | spl | spl | spl | spl | spl | spl |

**H** = Hit    **S** = Stand    **D** = Double    **spl** = Split
Do not split 55 and 10s. Always split 88 and AA.

## Master Chart Strategy Reminder

We have now covered the Basic Strategies you will find in most casinos. These are the foundation of any winning strategy, including card counting strategies.

To be a winner, you must make all the right strategy moves all the time.

# THE WINNING EDGE

Okay, you've gone through a lot of the material so far and are anxious to beat the casino. So you ask: "What will give me the winning edge? How can I beat the casino at blackjack?"

Let's go over that. The very first requirement is that you must perfectly understand and correctly *play* the Basic Strategies. Blackjack is a game where you're working to get a small edge over the casino. You cannot afford to give anything back to the casino and must play by the book, avoiding hunches, guesses and anything else that takes you away from the optimal strategies of the game.

Every play you make must be exactly as it should be. For example, when the dealer shows a 10 as an upcard, you must hit with 16, and with that very same 16, you need to stand if the dealer is showing a 4.

If you only make the right play sometimes, or usually, then you are not going to have a chance at winning long term. Sure, you may have some good sessions, but when you play poorly you give the casino the edge, and they *will* grind you down. Just give them time. Time works for the prepared player and against the ill-prepared one.

So that is step number one. Learn the Basic Strategies until you know them cold. I cannot repeat this dictum often enough.

Steps 2 and 3, as we discussed earlier in this book, are emotional control and money management. I have stressed over and over again in this book that they are vital to the winning formula.

### Understanding Card Counting

Basic Strategy players enjoy a very close game against the casino. If you play the Basic Strategy perfectly, you are among the best blackjack players in the casino. In single deck play with Las Vegas Strip Rules, the house has no edge on you! In multiple deck games, due to less sensitivity of particular card removal, the house enjoys about a 1/2% edge, a small edge that can be overcome by some advanced techniques used in conjunction with the Basic Strategy.

Computer studies have determined that 10s and Aces are the most valuable cards for the player, while the small cards, 2s through 7s, are the most valuable for the house, 8s and 9s being relatively neutral.

All counting systems base their winning strategies on keeping track of the ratio of high cards to low cards. The systems vary in complexity from the very simple to the very complicated, all being based on the same principle – betting more when there is a higher proportion of 10s and Aces in the deck, and less when there is a higher proportion of low cards, 2s through 7s, remaining.

If you want to further your edge over the casino and increase your winnings, you must learn either a counting system or the advanced non-counter strategy. See the back of the book for information on how to obtain the highly effective but simple to use *Cardoza Base Count Strategy,* the full *Home Instruction Course,* or the *Cardoza 1, 2, 3 Multiple Deck Non-Counter.*

Should you decide to improve your game further by learning a counting strategy, the strategies I've presented in this book are essential to know. They are the basis of *all* winning strategies.

The optimal basic strategies for all deck games that I have presented in this book are 100% correct and the absolute best available.

# UNDERSTANDING THE GAMBLE

One of the realities of any gambling proposition is that no matter how well you play the game, if chance is involved there will be times when you will experience terrible runs of bad luck. There is no way to predict when these runs will begin, how long they will last or when they will stop.

It is important to understand that just because you have an advantage over the house, it does not mean you will win every time. Having a bad losing streak is not necessarily a reflection on your playing abilities. Even the best players take beatings on occasion. With a small advantage in blackjack, the skillful player will be vulnerable to dizzying streaks of luck, both good and bad.

However, if a skill factor is involved in the gambling proposition, as it is in blackjack, that factor will eventually make the skillful player a winner. In the short run, luck goes back and forth, but as more and more hands get played out, skill begins to take its due and that is why it's so important to follow our winning strategies to the letter. Luck evens out in the long run, and when that is said and done, it is the skill of the player that will determine winning and losing.

For example, let's say you flip a coin and heads comes up five times in a row. Are those reflective of the true odds of flipping a head? Of course not. But flip that coin 1000 times, or even better, 10,000 times, and you can bet that the odds will be very close to 50-50, with either heads or tails, holding a slight edge. It all evens out in the long run.

The bettor that sticks by his guns when things go poorly will find tremendous rewards when things go his way, for in the end, a player with the skills of winning will be way ahead of the game, a big winner!

One more item we should discuss here. Gambling is fun for some players, but for others it is not fun, it is a problem. If you have a gambling problem, and are unable to stay away from the tables, get some professional help. Don't gamble with money you cannot afford to lose or that emotionally, really hurts you to lose. If this is the case, you don't belong at the tables for any amount of money, even pennies.

# EMOTIONAL CONTROL

It is important to recognize that behind every bet you make is *your* money and *your* emotions. Don't underestimate the importance of feeling positive when you play. The ups and downs of your moods and feelings affect the quality of your play. For blackjack to be a pleasurable and successful experience every time you gamble, you must be aware of your state of mind and obey its needs.

Sometimes you won't feel 100%. Perhaps your confidence or concentration is low. Maybe you're just not into gambling this particular day. Accept and recognize that condition and you will be doing yourself a favor.

Whenever you feel emotionally unprepared to lose money, my advice is to refrain from playing. You won't play as well as you could or should because your mind is not prepared for the stress of losing hands. Perhaps even more important than this is that you will receive no emotional satisfaction from the game. Just the opposite in fact. The game will be a drain. Hey, that's not what you're trying to do at the tables. We both know that.

Any time that the game of blackjack or any other form of gambling becomes a cause of anxiety and ceases to be a form of entertainment, than really, what are you doing there? Take a break, whether that break be a few hours after a refreshing swim or nap, a whole day, or perhaps even a much longer period of time.

Do not return to the tables until your confidence is up and you're feeling like a winner. To give yourself the best chances of being a winner, you need to feel like a winner. This statement is true in just about any aspect of life, not just gambling. Feeling good about yourself is a prerequisite to achieving goals both large and small.

Let me sum this up for you. Feeling good and having confidence are good; they put you in a position to win. Feeling bad and not having confidence are bad. They put you behind the eight ball and at a disadvantage.

Let's tie up these thoughts of confidence, feeling good, and money risk into the most important statement I am going to make in this entire book:

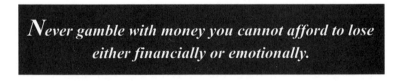

*Never gamble with money you cannot afford to lose either financially or emotionally.*

Never do this. Betting with money you cannot afford to lose is a guaranteed way to ensure yourself a losing career as a gambler, and to some extent, as a person.

From a financial viewpoint, the terrible havoc you can create by risking and losing food money, rent money, your kids college money, or whatever else that money was either earmarked for or could have achieved, has devastated families, marriages, careers and even lives. An untold number of foolish gamblers have destroyed themselves by chasing greed at the gaming tables.

That is the financial aspect, and it is no joking matter. But don't overlook the emotional aspects as well. There are many gamblers, and I see them every time I am in a casino setting, who just cannot handle losing a certain amount of money, yet they continue betting at unsafe levels. You have to avoid this kind of dangerous behavior and you do it by preparing your game plan before you even set foot in the casino.

I know this is all common sense, but it has been my experience that when it comes to gambling, most people throw that common sense out the window – along with their money.

Okay, let's move on to the bankroll issues.

# BANKROLLING

There are two bankroll issues you must think about when gambling, your total bankroll – how much you are comfortable risking, and your table bankroll – how much money you should bring to the table for any one session.

We will look at both these issues in this chapter.

## TOTAL BANKROLL

To be a successful blackjack player, your bankroll must be large enough to withstand the normal fluctuations common to blackjack. Under-capitalization and overbetting are great dangers to the serious gambler.

The player that consistently overbets will have larger winning sessions when he wins, but when he loses, he'll lose big and by definition, he'll lose too much. If a losing streak becomes extended, that player could get wiped out.

Playing with a bankroll large enough to sustain short swings of bad luck is the only way to insure that your skills will bear long term results. Get over it. You're going to lose sometimes, and sometimes you will continue to lose. That's part of the game. But you have to have enough around to still play.

I have formulated the following bankroll requirements to give you enough capital to survive any reasonable losing streak, and be able to bounce back on top.

In the following table, **flat** refers to betting the same amount every time and 1-4 refers to a bet spread of 1-4 units. Obviously, using a 1-4 spread will require more of a bankroll than flat betting since more money is put at risk

A **unit** represents the minimum bet, so if $5 is your minimum bet, and your bet range is 1-4, you would need $1,000 for a weekend's worth of play, as the chart below suggests. If you're only planning to play 10 hours at those stakes, $750 will give you a safe margin.

## TOTAL BANKROLL REQUIREMENTS

| Hours to Play | Bet Range | Bankroll Needed |
|---|---|---|
| 10 | Flat | 50 units |
| 20+ | Flat | 100 units |
| 10 | 1-4 | 150 units |
| 20+ | 1-4 | 200 units |

Do these numbers mean you will lose this much money? No but playing $5-$20, it is entirely possible just as it is possible that you could win that much or more. But you have to be prepared for eventualities that do occur in gambling. Losing streaks occur, and losing $500-$600 is a possibility when you're betting $5-$20 per hand.

If the thought of losing amounts comparable to this during

a downswing scares you, don't play $5-$20 a hand. That's betting over your head. Playing $25 and higher, obviously, the losing amounts can be even greater.

Again, bet within your financial and emotional means, and you will never regret a single session at the tables.

If you have a definite amount of money to play with and want to figure out how much your unit size bet should be, simply take your gambling stake and divide it by the amount of units you need to have.

Thus, if you bring $500 with you and plan to play for 10 hours ranging your bets from 1-4, divide $500 by 150 units and you will wager about $3 a hand. (See the Bankroll Needed column in the previous chart.) Betting more than $3 per unit would be overbetting, and leaving yourself vulnerable to the risks discussed earlier.

## TABLE BANKROLL

How much money should you bring to the table?

My recommendation is that your bring 30 units to the table each time you play. This doesn't mean you have to put the whole wad on the table at one time, but do have it available as a loss limit for the session. If that amount gets lost, quit, you have reached your one session limit.

If playing $5 units, bring $150; if $25 units, bring $750. $100 bettors would want to have $3,000 available. Take a look at the chart on the following page.

## TABLE BANKROLL RECOMMENDATIONS
### Bet Range: 1-4 Units

| Unit Bet | Minimum Stake | Maximum Stake |
| --- | --- | --- |
| $1 | $20 | $30 |
| $2 | $40 | $60 |
| $5 | $100 | $150 |
| $10 | $200 | $300 |
| $25 | $500 | $750 |
| $50 | $1000 | $1500 |
| $100 | $2000 | $3000 |

You can bring less if you want. If flat betting, that is, betting the same amount on every hand, 15 units will suffice. If your bet range is from 1-4 units, then 20 units will do the trick. However, do not bring more money to the table. 30 units is enough to cover normal swings, and you never want to lose more than that in any one sitting.

# WHEN TO QUIT

What often separates the winners from the losers is that the winners, when winning, leave the table a winner, and when losing, restrict their losses to affordable amounts. Smart gamblers never allow themselves to get destroyed at the table.

As a player, you have one big advantage the casino doesn't have - you can quit playing *anytime* you want to. This is a powerful weapon at your disposal, one that is implemented with great success by the really astute players.

To come out ahead, you must minimize your losses when losing and maximize your gains when winning. If you follow this sage advice, your winning sessions will eclipse your losing sessions and you will come out an overall winner.

How many times have you seen your friends, other players at your table, or even yourself, manage to turn a great session into an absolute disaster? Every inexperienced player goes through these situations, walking away afterwards and exclaiming in frustration and anger, "I should have quit!" And the problem is not with just inexperienced players and beginners; many experienced players get nailed as well.

It's a terrible feeling to be up $800 and cruising on cloud nine, and then suddenly, in a whirlwind of smoke and bad luck, you find yourself looking at a $200 hole, and then, $500, and then $1,000. It's no fun, it's painful, and it can certainly ruin the night. And it was completely avoidable. It not only didn't have to happen, it *shouldn't* have happened.

Equally bad is trying to play catch-up after a streak of bad luck by greatly increasing bets, and *hoping* a few good wins brings you right back in the game. That is dangerous, my friend, and how multitudes of players really get hurt in gambling.

The scenario above points out two sides of the money management coin you must get under control. The first part illustrates the problem of not walking away a winner, while the second part shows how the player ignored any type of stop-loss strategy, so necessary for the winning formula.

Let's look at each concept in turn and show you how to protect yourself against these catastrophes.

## MAXIMIZING GAINS

There are going to be times when you can do no wrong. Everything goes green for you. Your sixteens draw out into 20s and 21s, every double down is a winner, blackjacks are coming like you're an ace magnet, and the dealer busts every time you need him to. You're feeling like a genius and the chips are piling up.

But it won't last forever. The tide that was coming in, can

start going out at any time. And in a hurry.

What to do? Play smart. That's what you have to do.

Following are two tried and true steps to maximize your winning sessions at blackjack.

## 1. Once winning, the most important thing is to walk away a winner.

There is no worse feeling than to leave the table a loser after having been up a lot of money.

Once your wins at a table have exceeded 20 units, put aside 10 units of your winnings, and play the other 10 units. If a losing streak ensues and you lose those 10 units, you have protected yourself. You walk away with 10 units in winnings!

If you're a more aggressive player, you can make those numbers 30 units before putting the chips away, and 20 units as the bottom. Then walk.

Enjoy a night on the town, using your winnings for a little something extra. But under no circumstances do you give back that money!

## 2. Set no limit on your winning sessions.

If your hot streak continues, keep putting wins aside into your "don't touch" pile. When your luck changes and you have lost that 10 unit buffer, you can quit a big winner.

## Should you increase your bet size when winning?

If you would like to try for a bigger win, the answer is

yes, go for it - but in moderation. Do not get overzealous for that leaves your hard-earned win vulnerable to a few big losses. Increase your bets gradually when winning, keeping in mind that the more you bet, the more you risk losing.

One more thing to keep in mind. Just because you may have won six hands in a row doesn't mean that you'll win your seventh bet. You can just as easily lose that seventh hand as you could win it.

The theory on betting more at "hot" tables sounds good, but nobody has ever made a living following that strategy. Mathematically, and in practice, only the odds of the game determine a player's chances of winning a particular play, not the won or lost results from a previous play.

## MINIMIZING LOSSES
Even more important than protecting your wins is protecting your bankroll. It is easy to get carried away at the tables, and in anger, frustration, or blind hope, end up digging a hole so deep, you have little chance of coming back.

We've all been there, in one form or another. The key: Never put yourself in that situation again..

Here are three simple guidelines that, if followed, will save you a lot of money.

### 1. Limit your table losses to 20 units.
If betting $5 chips, never lose more than $100 in any one session; if $2 units, then $40; if $25 units, then $500.

Again, as in the Maximizing Wins section, aggressive players can bump this up to 30 units, but that should be the limit. Chasing lost money after a bad losing session is really bad news.

Do not dig in for more money, and you can never be a big loser. Take a break, try again later. You never want go get into a position where losing so much in one session totally demoralizes you.

## 2. Never increase your bet range beyond your bankroll capabilities.

In other words, always bet within your means. If you're a $25 chip player, you have no business betting $100 chips, and if you're a $5 player, playing those greens can put a hurt on you in a hurry. Gambling is supposed to be a form of entertainment, or profit, not a field to test your masochistic tendencies or hurt yourself financially.

## 3. Never increase your bet size to catch up and break even.

Raising your bets will not change the odds of the game, nor will it change your luck. What it will do is make your chances of taking a terrible beating frighteningly high. Do not get into a position where losing so much in one session destroys any reasonable chance of coming out even. You can't win all the time.

As I said earlier, even I don't win all the time, but the times I lose, I keep it within reason. I'll be coming back to get them next time, full of confidence, and playing my best game. And that's what makes me so hard to beat.

Remember, you're on a mission to take the casino's money and come home flashing those pearly whites. Keep that in mind champ.

# WHEN TO QUIT II

In this chapter, we will look at five situations that commonly occur at the blackjack table. These are situations I am frequently asked about and see all too often at the table. The advice here continues the theme of the last three chapters, taking hold of and understanding how your emotions affect your playing, and acting upon them in a wise manner.

Let's start with one of the most frequently asked questions: What do you do about bad players at your table?

## SITUATION # 1
### Playing with Bad Players
Players simply hate playing with other players who draw when they should stand or stand when they should draw, particularly when the results of that decision cause their own hand to lose. I frequently hear this complaint from players who describe how much money they lost due to the bad play of their tablemate.

For some players, nothing is more annoying than sitting on the table with a 16 against the dealer's 5, and watching with horror as the third basemen draws on his own 14 – as opposed to standing – and busts out with a 10. Meanwhile, the dealer flops over a 9 for a 14, and rather than

103

drawing the 10 already taken by the inept third baseman, proceeds instead to draw a 7 for a perfect 21, busting out the whole table and causing a rippling of mumbling and anger from the other players.

It is bad enough for the player holding the 15, how about the other player who holds a 20! Ouch!

But you know what? It doesn't matter what any player does or how bad they are. It makes absolutely no difference to your chances of winning. Absolutely none. I personally couldn't care less if I was playing with a bunch of monkeys.

In the long run, whether you have a good fundamentals player behind you or the bozo from bozoland who turns every hand into an adventure, the truth is that *mathematically*, this player has no effect on your winning or losing chances.

Bad plays that cost money will really stick out to you at the table. However, the reality is that you probably won't notice or remember the other side of the coin, the times that the "bozo" bad play helped you win a big hand.

You know what? It all equals out in the long run. Bad players help as often as they hurt. Stop worrying about them. How could you possible know what card they will take? However, if bad players disturb your enjoyment of the game or your concentration, move to another table. If you are more worried about someone else's play than your own, obviously a change of scenery is in order.

## SITUATION # 2
**You've Just Lost Two Big Bets and Are Really Angry**
As we all know, losing is as much a part of gambling as winning. But what separates the smart players from the casino cannon fodder is how one deals with losing and that is what we are going to discuss here.

Emotions can often be hard to control, but what you can control, are your actions when a situation upsets your state of balance. When a car cuts someone off, that person tends to get angry. There are different ways a person can express this anger from a relatively mild honking of the horn, to a more aggressive cursing or finger flipping response, all the way to an extreme violent retribution. None of these responses have any positive value at all. In fact, they only create the potential for even bigger problems with no positive resolution in any of the scenarios.

My point: It's how you deal with this situation. Okay, you lost a few bad hands and you are angry. Anger clouds judgment, and like the driving situation, it can cause a "retaliatory" large bet, or equally damaging, fear of the needed and proper aggressive play. Correct double downs and splits may not be made, and hitting and standing decisions get subject to reasoning that has nothing to do with correct blackjack play.

Anger and frustration caused by losing takes enjoyment out of the game and leads to poor decision-making. The two feed off each other, both hastening a losing skid and worsening the experience.

Let me point out the obvious move here. Take a break!

Get away from the tables and take a walk, catch a meal, whatever. But get away from the table. No good can come out of chasing losing bets.

This leads us to the next situation – chasing bets.

## SITUATION # 3
### Chasing Lost Bets and Losing Sessions

Losing sessions happen and there is nothing you can do about them. It is the *big* losing sessions, the ones that really destroy you that can be prevented – all the time. There is no excuse for letting yourself get pounded flat. At that point, it is not bad luck. It is bad judgment.

Chasing bad bets and bad sessions with bigger bets is the worst thing you can do at the tables. Making larger bets won't suddenly create a winning streak. What it can do is make you lose at a faster, harder and more horrifying pace, one that can often feed on itself into dizzying depths.

Accept your losses and take a walk. It's okay to lose. You can always come back. It's not okay however, to lose wildly, because the only way to come back from a gigantic loss is to set yourself up for an even bigger fall, one that may have bigger implications in your life than what you expected before you sat down at the table.

## SITUATION # 4
### You Keep Losing Your Big Double Downs

It happens my friend, as you well know. You get burned a few times, and you're snakebit, afraid to make the next one. You'll win some, you'll lose some. But any time you become hesitant or afraid to make the proper aggressive play, then you are not at your best and it is time for a breather. It's never good to play scared.

## SITUATION # 5
### Getting Angry or Distracted by Bad Luck

Anytime, and I mean anytime, that you have lost your composure at the table – for whatever reason – then it's time to walk from the tables. Going on *tilt*, a poker term indicating a person is angry and not playing their best game, is never good in gambling, whether in poker where the other players feast off the tilted player's emotional and inferior play, or in blackjack, where the house benefits from poor judgment.

I don't care what took you off center. Once your concentration is gone or you're emotionally off center, hey baby, it's time to get some air.

# GENERAL ADVICE

A common trap you need to protect yourself against is the temptation to deviate from correct strategy. This can happen for a variety of reasons, but whatever the reason – superstition, a hunch, or some painful losses – when you start making strategy decisions on any basis other than the mathematically correct Basic Strategy, that is when you start giving the edge back to the house.

You must avoid getting distracted by the small picture at blackjack. What happened on the last draw or last few draws, whether you won or lost the last few hands, or the disheartening times when a dealer draws out to a 21 on a hand you thought was locked up, have no bearing on your chances of winning the next hand.

The cards have not suddenly taken on a brain. They are inanimate objects. Win or lose the previous hand, the strategy *never* changes in blackjack. There is only one correct way to play.

I have seen this time and time again. "Well," a player might say, "the strategy didn't work on that play. I really should have stuck with my instincts and played that hand the way I wanted to."

Danger! The hunch player has arrived! Casinos feast off hunch players as well as the lucky charmers, the superstitious ones, and all the other bad thinking that grows like bad algae in a pool. Once, the algae starts muddying up your water, so to speak, the casino has got you.

It is easy to fall into these traps. It happens to just about everyone so in this chapter, I am going to crawl into your head for a little bit and try to get you thinking straight about how to deal with your money in a casino.

**Streaks as a Predictor of the Next Hand**
Streaks and recent events have no bearing on what the correct strategy should be for any given situation. It does not matter that you may have won the last five hands. It says nothing about what will happen the next five hands or even the very next one.

If you have won five hands in a row, are you on a streak? Of course. Will it continue? If you answer yes to that question and knew that yes to be a true statement, then you would have to be a complete fool not to drag your home mortgage, all your jewelry and life savings, your car, and any spare money you could dig up from every friend and relative you had, and get it onto the felt circle at the table.

And if the answer is not yes, but a "maybe I don't know," as I hope that answer will be, then get off the notion of a streak as a predictor of future behavior. The cold hard truth is that none of us are psychics – we cannot predict what will happen to a deck of cards with any more accuracy than anyone else.

If you feel lucky, or that you are on a streak that will continue, it is okay to increase your bet *moderately*. You can't get hurt by a gradual increase of bets. You can however, get hurt badly by a large increase over your normal bet size. If your hunch is wrong, one overly large bet that loses can turn a big winning session into a losing one of nightmarish proportions in a big hurry.

One large losing bet can quickly turn into a series of larger losing bets as you desperately chase. Boom, boom, boom, what happened? One minute you're winning solidly and feeling good. The next minute, after a fateful large bad turned sour, and then another and another, you are suddenly in big trouble, and before you know it, you just want to hide your head in a hole. Be careful ostrich! Bets out of proportion to your betting can easily turn one or two hours of a winning effort into a night to forget.

Get the picture? Avoid playing streaks with anything but gradual increases. Nobody knows how the next few hands will fall.

**Protecting Good Hands Against Blackjacks**
Many players feel the need to protect their 19s, 20s, and blackjacks when the dealer shows an Ace for an upcard and asks in that sweet tilting voice, "Insurance?" This is bad short term thinking.

Insurance is a terrible bet regardless of whether you hold a blackjack, a 20 or a 15. Let me put it to you a different way. If you took insurance out every time the dealer showed an ace, on those insurance bets, you would lose at a faster rate than just about any other gamble offered in the casino, way faster than even double zero roulette with its big house edge of 5.26%. That's how bad a bet insurance is.

## Drinking at the Table

Should you drink and play at the same time? There are two ways to look at this. If you're a serious gambler, the answer is always "no." If you're a casual gambler trying to win, the answer is a qualified no. I say "qualified," because I understand that you want to have fun while playing and it is hard to pass up free anything, especially free drinks when you are on vacation or just out to have a good time.

If one drink won't affect your play, maybe two, go for it. Have a little fun. *But don't have too much fun.* It's more fun to leave a winner than leave a loser. I think we can all agree on that. Why stack the odds against yourself? Even better, when you're ready to depart the table, order up a few drinks and take them to go.

Don't lose any sleep about passing up those free drinks at the table. You know what? It will be much cheaper if you pay for those drinks at the bar *after* you finish gambling. I think you know what I am talking about.

Alcohol impairs judgment and clear thinking, and if you don't think that is the case, you should probably go directly from this sentence and straight to the head doctor. Drinking may be all fun and good, but if you've got money on the line and take that money seriously, why would you impair your thinking and give the house an unfair advantage?

People that are drinking can't think straight, they play too long, they make bad decisions, they are prone to overbet, and any chance they had at making sound money management decisions gets drowned in that cocktail glass. All these things are bad for you and good for the casino. Why do you think all those nice drinks are supplied *gratis* by the casino?

Conclusion: It's not smart to drink and gamble.

## BAD HAND TEMPTATIONS

It is easy for players to get superstitious in this game, and as a result, deviate from the proper Basic Strategy plays. This can happen for a number of reasons and lead to bad playing decisions, what I call "bad hand temptations."

Let's look at one of these situations.

### 16 vs. 10 and 15 vs. 10

How often do you get saddled with those 15s and 16s when the dealer shows a 10 and *just know* you are going to get that 10 and bust? Pretty often, I'm sure. And you're thinking you have a better chance of staying in the hand with a lousy hand than committing hari-kari by busting.

Well guess what? First, you don't *know* that you are going to get a 10 and bust. Second, you don't have a better chance of winning by standing and that is why you need to take a card. Let me explain further.

When you are dealt a 16 and the dealer is facing you with a mighty 10, you aren't looking pretty. Whether you take a card or not, you will probably lose, and you will lose often to the tune, on average, of about 75% of the time. That is a lot.

Simply put, you've been dealt a bad hand and now have to make the best of it. Look at it another way. Let's say you're trapped in a dark alley and are attacked by some thug twice your size. You're not too optimistic about the situation, but just the same, you are going to do your best. If you could put a bet down, it wouldn't be on yourself because you don't like your chances. But at the same time, you have a better chance of defending yourself with a trick or two you might try, than meekly giving in.

It's the same when you hold a 15 versus the dealer's upcard of 10. You have a losing situation. While drawing is bad, standing is even worse. You just have to give yourself the best chances of winning, that's all. Don't expect to win here, but at the same time, do everything you can to improve your chances.

**Hunches and Feelings,**
As discussed throughout this book, there is only *one* correct way to play any given situation. There is no opinion on what is right. Either the decision is right, or it is not right. End of story. If you have a 13 and the dealer holds a 10, the correct play is to hit. There are no other correct plays.

If you want to play by hunches, feelings, intuition or whatever else, than you are wasting time by reading this book.

I am here to show you how to win money at blackjack, not cater to ideas you have about how to win money. Your opinions, or any one else's for that matter, are worthless. Blackjack is a mathematical game, every situation has a clear-cut correct answer. Save your opinions for politics or sports, areas outside the mathematical realm, where there are debatable issues. In blackjack, it is all black and white.

If you think you or someone else you know has that special voodoo where they can predict hands, cards, or winning and losing streaks, then send them my way my friend and I will gladly play the casino.

Let me say this again. There is no voodoo at this game, hunches are worthless, and opinions are as valuable to your chances of winning as a straw hat is for a polar bear. In blackjack, there is only one correct way to play any given situation. Period.

# THE MYTH OF CARD COUNTING

There are so many misconceptions about card counting and what it takes not only to beat the casino at single deck blackjack, but multiple deck as well, that I had to devote a small chapter to this topic. It is time to directly address all the false notions players have about card counting.

Do multiple decks stop card counters as casinos intended? Not at all. Of all the misconceptions about blackjack, and there are many, the biggest misconception of all is that it is hard to count cards in a multiple deck. On the contrary, it is easy to count cards, whether it be a single deck or a multiple deck. And with the landmark non-counting multiple deck strategy that I developed in the 90's, it is even possible to beat the multiple deck game without a counting strategy.

Blackjack can be beat – with the odds. One deck, four decks, whatever, there is still no casino that will knowingly deal cards to me. And it's not because casinos don't like the green of my money. They just don't like me getting their green.

Card counting is fairly simple, so simple in fact that just about anyone can learn how to count cards in under one hour. The term "card counting" is actually misleading because you are not actually counting cards, but keeping just one number in your head – that's it. Essentially, that one number tells you whether there are more high cards in the deck than low cards, which is good for you, or whether there are more low cards than high ones, which is good for the casino.

The simplicity of counting cards comes as a shock to just about everyone I have taught, but again, that is only if you use a system that is designed for use under *actual* casino conditions, and one that is a legitimate one – two conditions that were hard to find when I originally developed the Cardoza Base Count Strategy. You don't need to be mathematically oriented or even have a particularly good memory to be a counter. You do need, however, to be willing to invest some time to become a winning player.

My students can never get over it when I have them counting cards within five minutes and using the strategy within one hour. It's really that simple. If you take your money seriously and don't like losing, I strongly encourage you to learn a counting strategy, or if you are not so inclined, our non-counting strategy, the Cardoza 1,2,3 Multiple Deck Non-Counter.

Either way, the gain in your skills will pay for the strategies in under an hour. The ads in the back of this book will let you know more about them, but keep in mind that these strategies are only available at Cardoza Publishing – we don't sell these to any outside vendor.

# GLOSSARY

**Barring a Player** - The exclusion of a player from the blackjack tables.

**Basic Strategy** - The optimal playing strategy for a particular set of rules and number of decks used, assuming the player has knowledge of only his own two cards and the dealer's upcard.

**Blackjack or Natural** - An original two card holding consisting of an Ace and ten-value card. Also the name of the game.

**Break** - see Bust.

**Burn Card** - A card, usually form the top of the deck, that is removed from play. The top card is traditionally *burned* after a fresh shuffle and before the cards are dealt.

**Bust or Break** - To exceed the total of 21, a loser.

**Card Counting** - A method of keeping track of the cards already played so that knowledge of the remaining cards can be used to adjust strategies. A player that counts cards is called a *card counter*.

**Composition of the Deck** - A term used to describe the particular makeup of the cards remaining in the deck.

**Composition Change** - As cards are removed from the deck, the normal proportion of certain cards to other groups of cards change. This is called a composition change.

**Dealer** - The casino employee who deals the cards, makes the proper payoffs to winning hands and collects lost bets.

**Doubling, Doubling Down** - A player option to double the original bet after seeing his original two cards. If the player chooses this option, one additional card will be dealt.

**Doubling after Splitting** - Option offered in only some United States and international casinos whereby players are allowed to double down after splitting a pair (according to normal doubling rules).

**Draw** - see Hit.

**Early Surrender** - An option to forfeit a hand and lose half the bet before the dealer checks for a blackjack.

**Exposed Card** - see Upcard.

**Eye in the Sky** - Refers to the mirrors above the gaming tables where the games are constantly supervised to protect both the player and the house from being cheated.

**Face Card** - Also known as **Paint**. A Jack, Queen or King.

**First Base** - Seat closest to the dealer's left. The first baseman acts upon his hand first.

**Flat Bet** - To bet the same amount every hand.

**Hard Total** - A hand without an Ace or if containing an Ace, where the Ace counts as only 1 point (10, 6, A).

QUICK GUIDE TO WINNING BLACKJACK

**Hit** - The act of drawing (requesting) a card from the dealer.

**Hole Card** - The dealer's unexposed downcard.

**House** - A term to denote the Casino.

**Insurance** - A side bet that can be made when the dealer shows an Ace. The player wagers up to half his original bet and gets paid 2 to 1 on that bet if the dealer shows a blackjack. If the dealer does not have a blackjack, the insurance bet is lost.

**Multiple Deck Game** - Blackjack played with two or more decks of cards, usually referring to a 4, 6 or 8 deck game.

**Natural** - see Blackjack.

**Nickels** - $5 chips, usually red in color.

**Pat Card** - A dealer upcard of 7 through Ace, that tends to give the dealer pat hands.

**Pat Hand** - A hand totaling 17-21.

**Pit Boss** - Casino employee who supervises play at the tables.

**Push** - A tie between the dealer and the player.

**Quarters** - $25 chips, usually green in color.

**Shoe** - An oblong box used to hold multiple decks of cards.

**Shuffle, Shuffling Up** - The mixing of cards by a dealer prior to a fresh round of play.

**Silver** - $1 tokens or dollar chips.

**Single Deck Game** - Blackjack played from a single pack of cards.

**Soft Hands, Soft Total** - Hand in which the Ace counts as 11 points.

**Splitting Pairs** - A player option to split two cards of identical value so that two separate hands are formed. A bet equal to the original wager is placed next to the second hand.

**Stand, Stand Pat** - A player's decision not to draw a card.

**Stiff Card** - A dealer upcard of 2 through 6, that leaves the dealer with a high busting potential.

**Stiff Hand** - A hand totaling hard 12, 13, 14, 15 or 16; can be busted if hit.

**Surrender, Late Surrender** - A player option to forfeit his original hand and lose half the bet after it has been determined that the dealer does not have a blackjack.

**Ten Factor** - Refers to the concentration of tens in the deck.

**Ten-Value Card** - 10, Jack, Queen or King.

**Third Base** - Also called **Anchorman.** Position closest to the dealer's right. The third baseman makes the last play before the dealer's turn.

**Toke or Tip** - A gratuity either given or bet for the dealer.

**Unit** - Bet size used as a standard of measurement.

**Upcard** - The dealer's face up (exposed) card.

# THE CARDOZA CRAPS MASTER
### Exclusive Offer! - Not Available Anywhere Else)
## Three Big Strategies!

Here It is! **At last**, the **secrets** of the **Grande-Gold Power Sweep, Molliere's Monte Carlo Turnaround** and the **Montarde-D'Girard Double Reverse** - three big strategies - are made available and presented for the **first time anywhere**! These powerful strategies are designed for the serious craps player, one wishing to bring the best odds and strategies to hot tables, cold tables and choppy tables.

### I. THE GRANDE-GOLD POWER SWEEP (HOT TABLE STRATEGY)

This **dynamic strategy** takes maximum advantage of hot tables and shows you how to amass small **fortunes quickly** when numbers are being thrown fast and furious. The Grande-Gold stresses aggressive betting on wagers the house has no edge on! This previously unreleased strategy will make you a powerhouse at a hot table.

### 2. MOLLIERE'S MONTE CARLO TURNAROUND (COLD TABLE STRATEGY)

For the player who likes betting against the dice, Molliere's Monte Carlo Turnaround shows how to turn a cold table into hot cash. Favored by an exclusive circle of professionals who will play nothing else, the uniqueness of this strongman strategy is that the vast majority of bets **give absolutely nothing away to the casino**!

### 3.MONTARDE-D'GIRARD DOUBLE REVERSE (CHOPPY TABLE STRATEGY)

This **new** strategy is the **latest development** and the **most exciting strategy** to be designed in recent years. **Learn how** to play the optimum strategies against the tables when the dice run hot and cold (a choppy table) with no apparent reason. **The Montarde-d'Girard Double Reverse** shows how you can **generate big profits** while less knowledgeable players are ground out by choppy dice. And, of course, the majority of our bets give nothing away to the casino!

### BONUS!!!

Order now, and you'll receive **The Craps Master-Professional Money Management Formula** ($15 value) **absolutely free**! Necessary for serious players and **used by the pros**, the **Craps Master Formula** features the unique **stop-loss ladder**.

**The Above Offer is Not Available Anywhere Else. You Must Order Here.**

To order send ~~$75~~ $50 (plus postage and handling) by check or money order to:
Cardoza Publishing, P.O. Box 1500, Cooper Station, New York, NY 10276

126

# WIN MONEY AT BLACKJACK! SPECIAL OFFER!
## THE CARDOZA BASE COUNT STRATEGY

**Finally**, a count strategy has been developed which allows the average player to play blackjack like a **pro**! Actually, this strategy isn't new. The Cardoza Base Count Strategy has been used successfully by graduates of the Cardoza School of Blackjack for years. But **now**, for the **first time**, this "million dollar" strategy, which was only available previously to those students attending the school, is available to **you**!

### FREE VACATIONS! A SECOND INCOME?
You bet! Once you learn this strategy, you will have the skills to **consistently win big money** at blackjack. The longer you play, the more you make. The casino's bankroll is yours for the taking.

### BECOME AN EXPERT IN TWO DAYS
Why struggle over complicated strategies that aren't as powerful? In just **two days or less**, you can learn the Cardoza Base Count and be among the best blackjack players. Friends will look up to you in awe - for you will be a **big winner** at blackjack.

### BEAT ANY SINGLE OR MULTIPLE DECK GAME
We show you how, with just a **little effort**, you can effectively beat any single or multiple deck game. You'll learn how to count cards, how to use advanced betting and playing strategies, how to make money on insurance bets, and much, much, more in this 6,000 word, chart-filled strategy package.

### SIMPLE TO USE, EASY TO MASTER
**You too can win!** The **power** of the Cardoza Base Count strategy is not only in its **computer-proven** winning results but also in its **simplicity**. Many beginners who thought card counting was too difficult have given the Cardoza Base Count the acid test - they have **won consistently** in casinos around the world.

The Cardoza Base Count strategy is designed so that **any player** can win under practical casino conditions. **No need** for a mathematical mind or photographic memory. **No need** to be bogged down by calculations. Keep **only one number** in your head at any time. The casinos will never suspect that you're a counter.

### DOUBLE BONUS!!
**Rush** your order in **now**, for we're also including, **absolutely free**, the 1,000 and 1,500 word essays, "How to Disguise the Fact that You're an Expert", and "How Not to Get Barred". Among other **inside information** contained here, you'll learn about the psychology of the pit bosses, how they spot counters, how to project a losing image, role playing, and other skills to maximize your profit potential.

As an **introductory offer to readers of this book**, the Cardoza Base Count Strategy, which has netted graduates of the Cardoza School of Blackjack **substantial sums** of **money**, is offered here for **only $50**! To order, send $50 by check or money order to:
Cardoza Publishing, P.O. Box 1500, Cooper Station, New York, NY 10276